Do you long for something more?
Do you hear the whispers of your heart nudging you?
These whispers encourage you to listen and pay attention.

Your longing for something more will subside as you
immerse yourself in a gentle journey.
A journey to discover your fearless self.

As with anything in life in order for it to grow and
blossom we need to nurture it.
As you color the pages in this book you will be nurturing
your creative spirit. You will find yourself in the now,
free of the regrets of the past and worries of tomorrow.

As you explore your sense of possibility the limits you
once placed on yourself will diminish.
Being "Free to fly" encourages you to be willing to let go of
any preconceived ideas of how you are supposed to be.

This is a safe place to explore.
A place to capture the essence of the child within.
A place to nurture the woman you may have lost along the way.
Do not worry you will awaken your beauty
as you express your-self with color.

Learn to be bold with color.
Allow yourself to have fun and play.
It is your birthright.
What colors make you smile?
What colors make your heart sing?

I hope this book inspires you to listen to the whispers
compelling you to live a creative, passionate life where
you discover hidden treasures that are full of your hopes
and dreams. To find the place where you feel "Free to fly".

By Laurie M. Kapalka

These drawings are meant for you to discover your

brilliance and express your creativity.

Feel free to share your works of art with me.

Enjoy !!!

Free to fly

choosewiselyfriends@outlook.com

Please post your completed colourings to my Facebook page

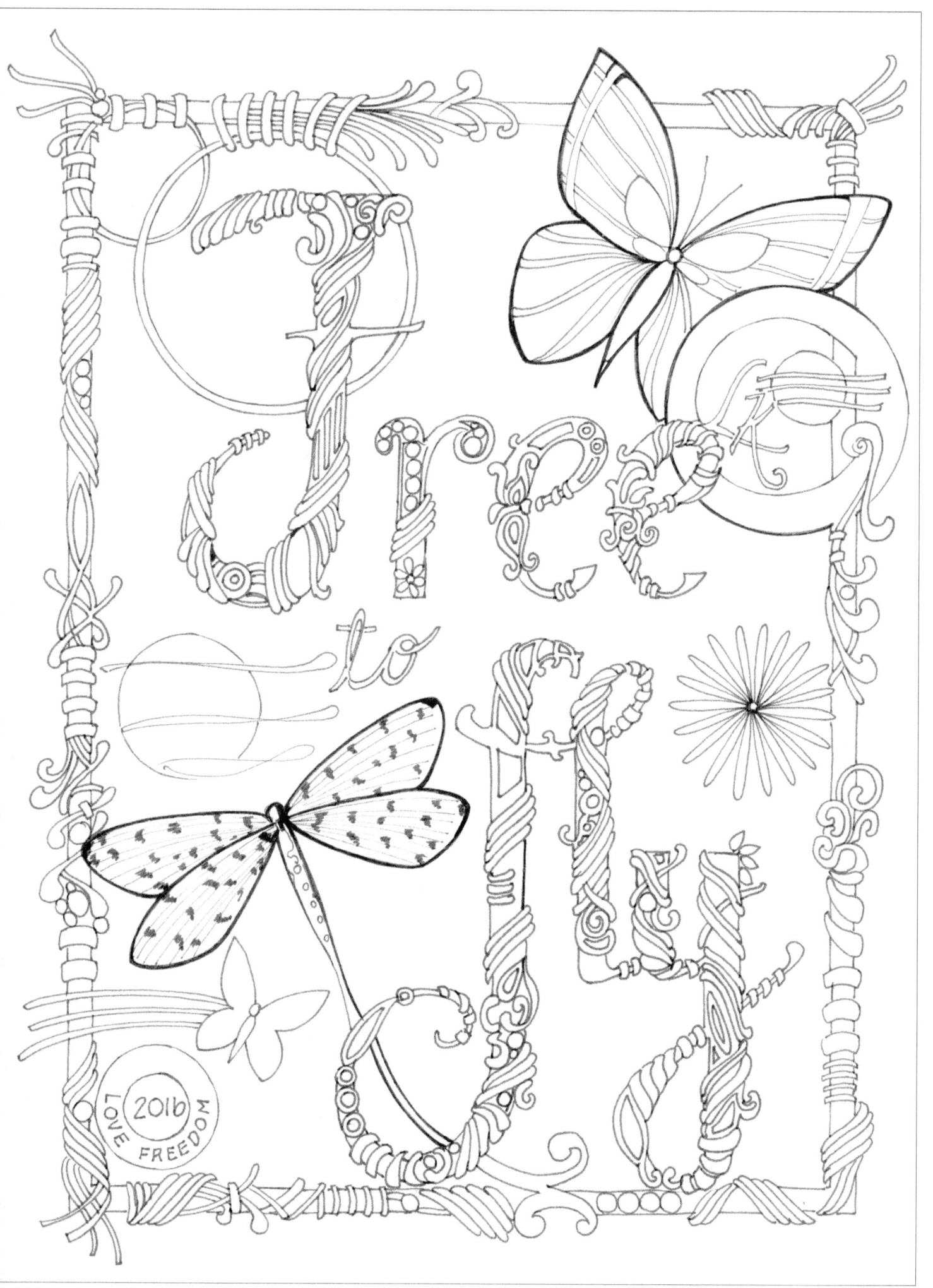

Free to fly

LOVE FREEDOM 2016

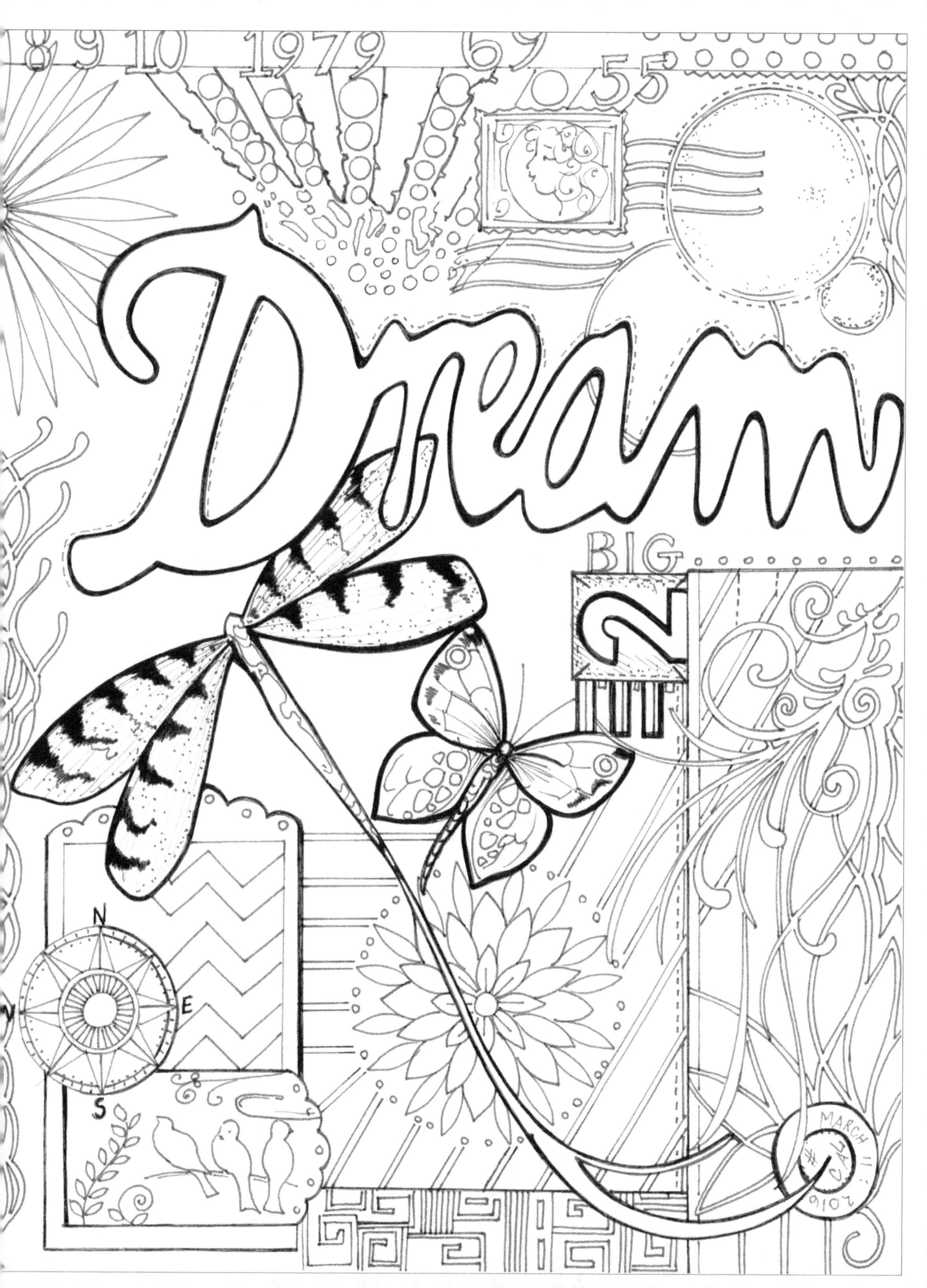

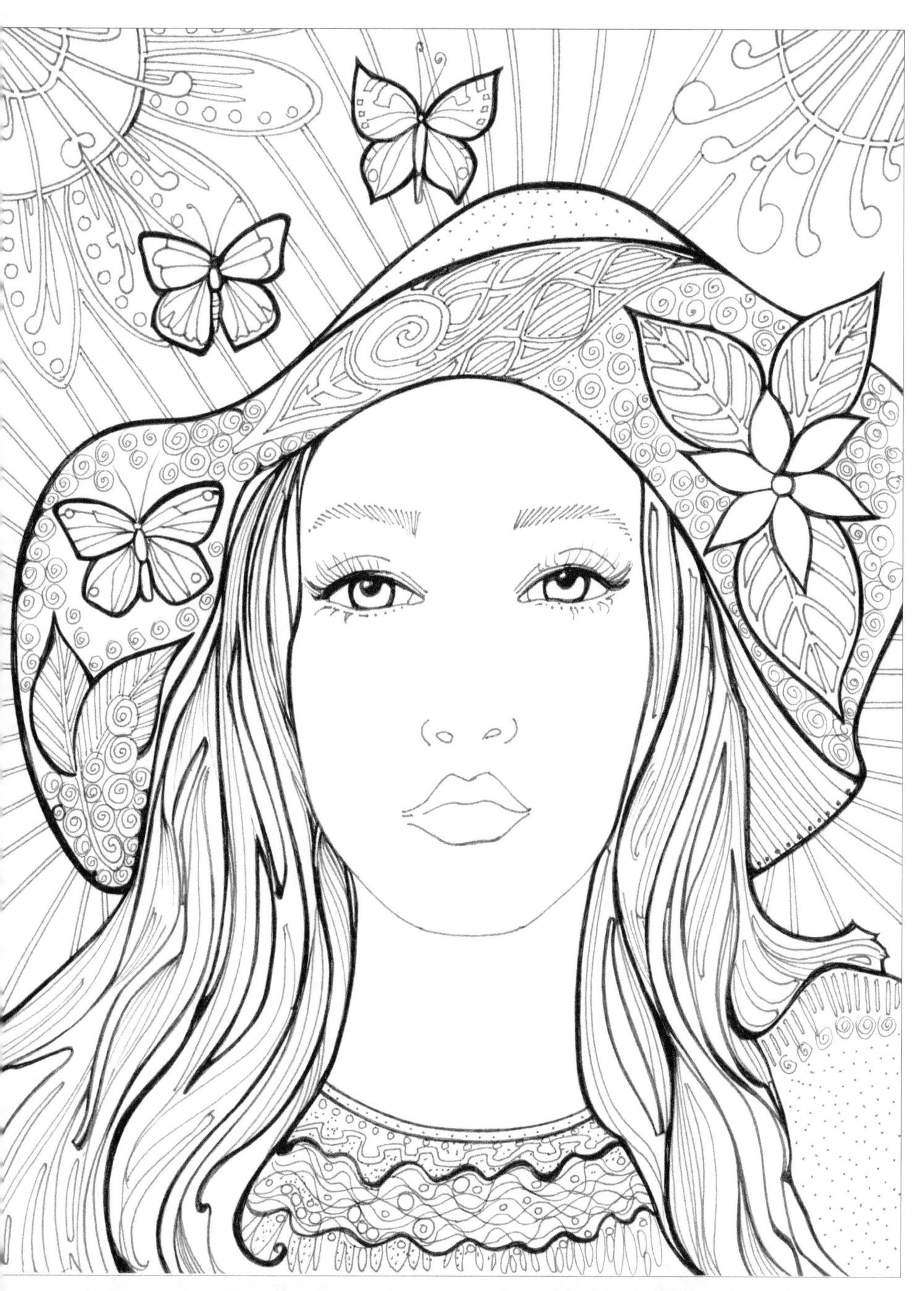

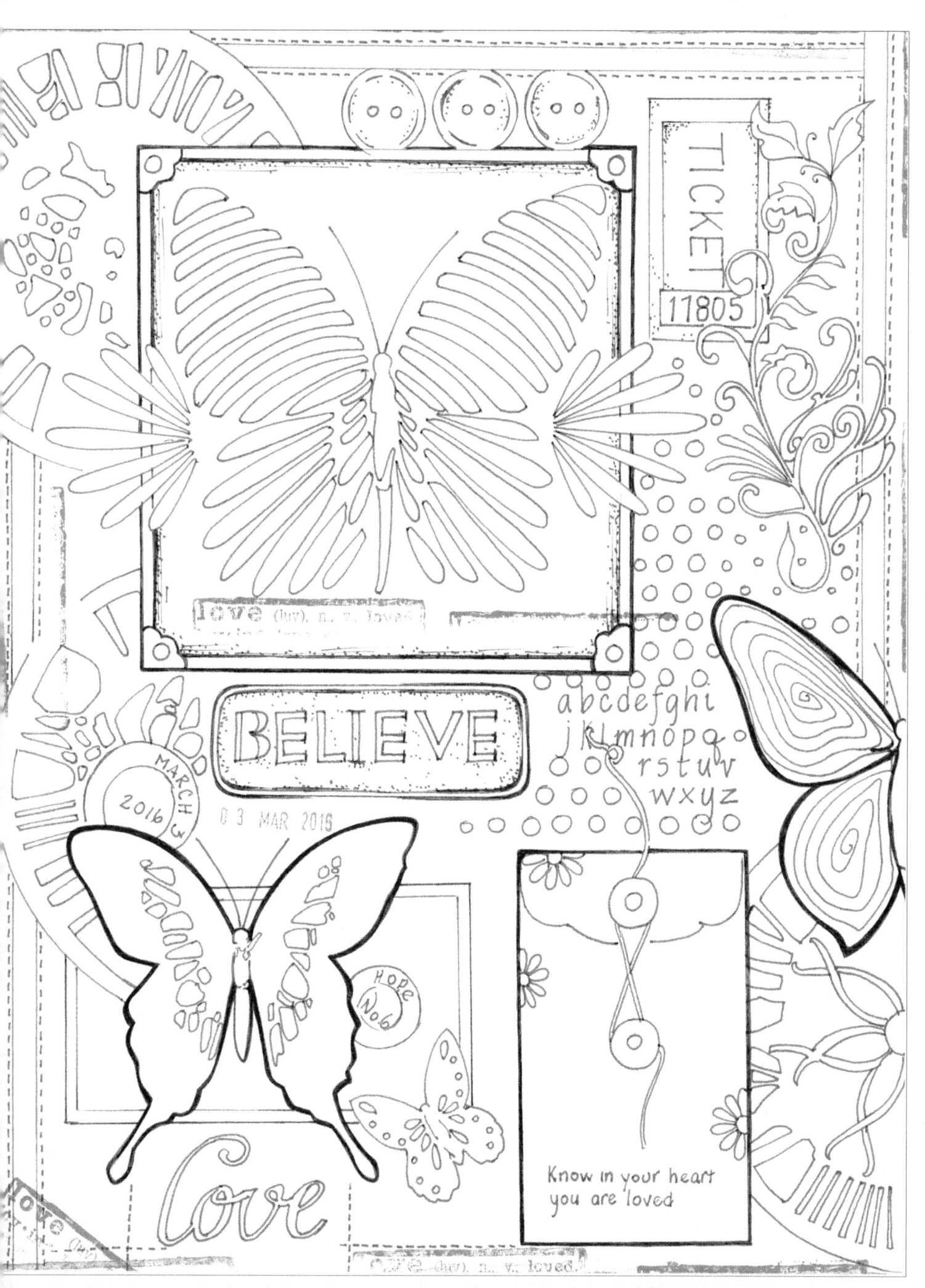

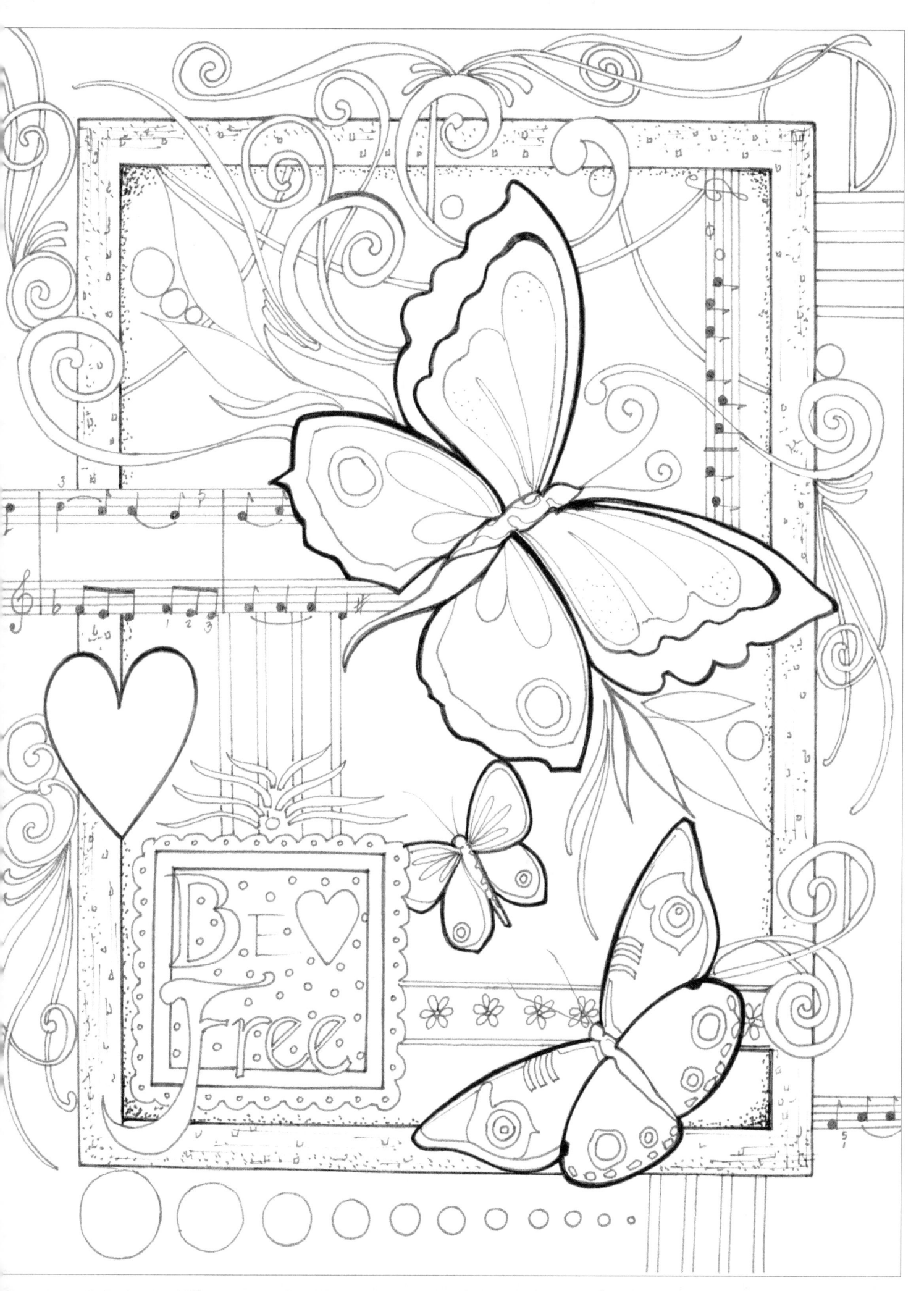

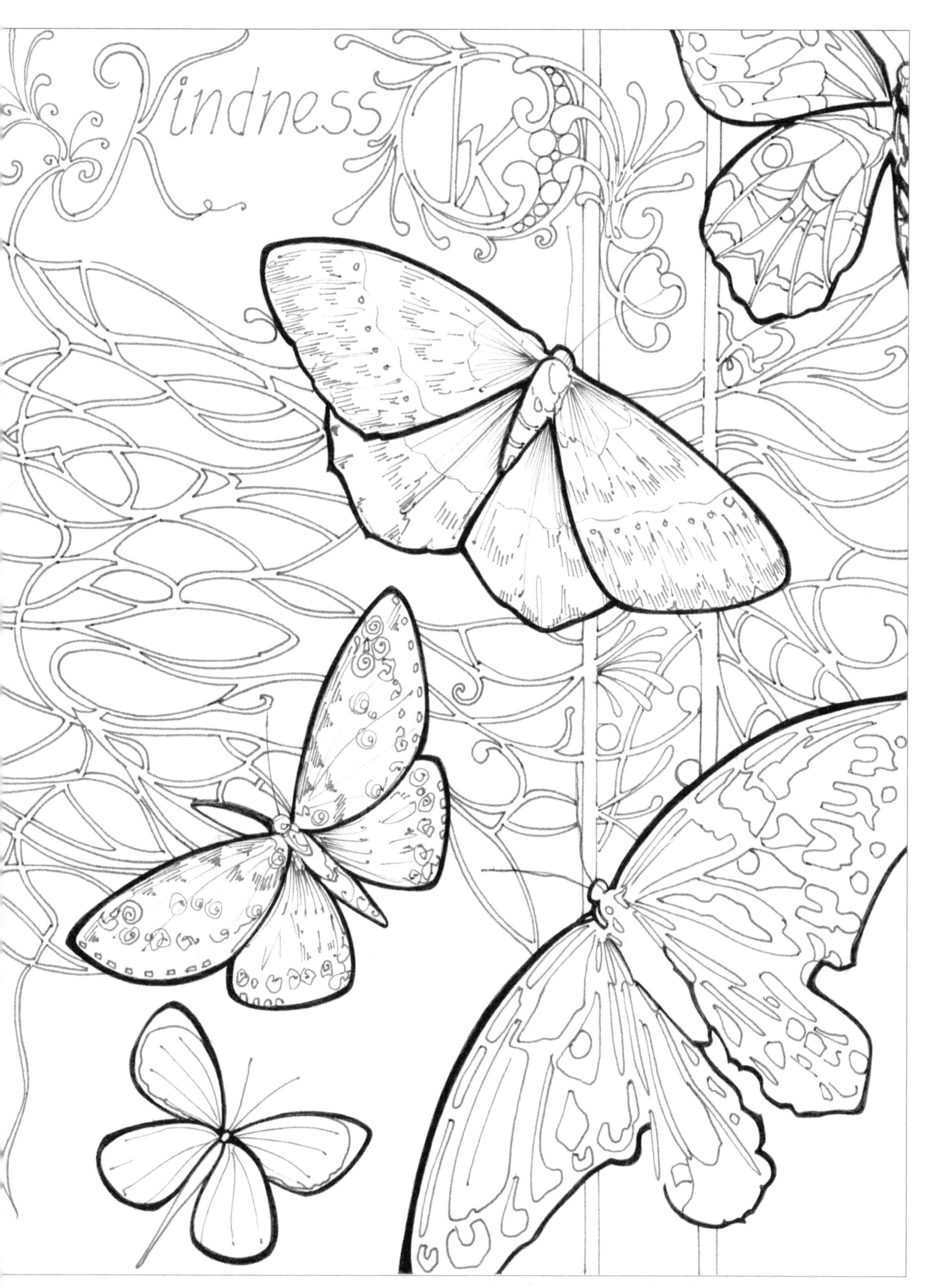

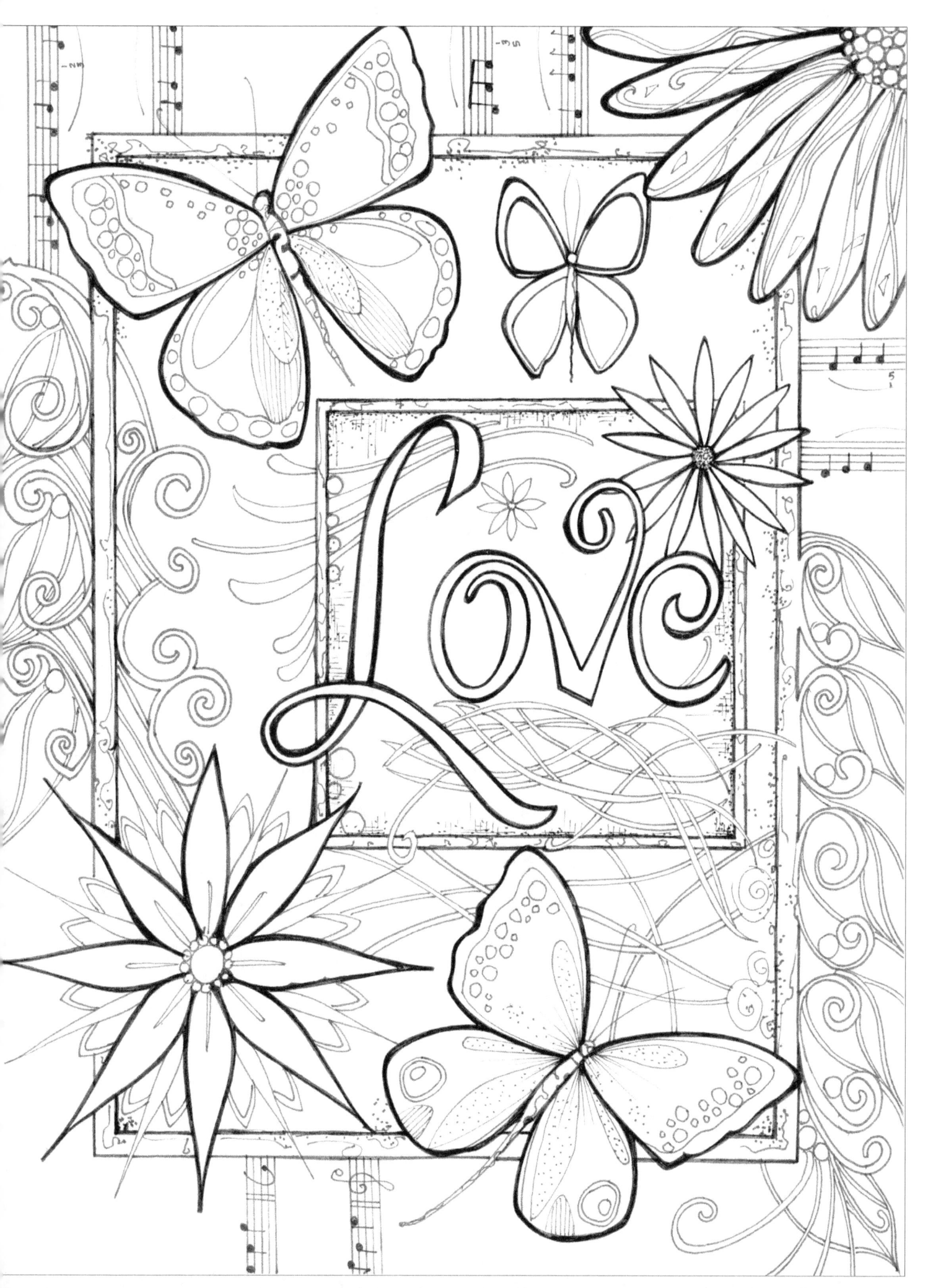

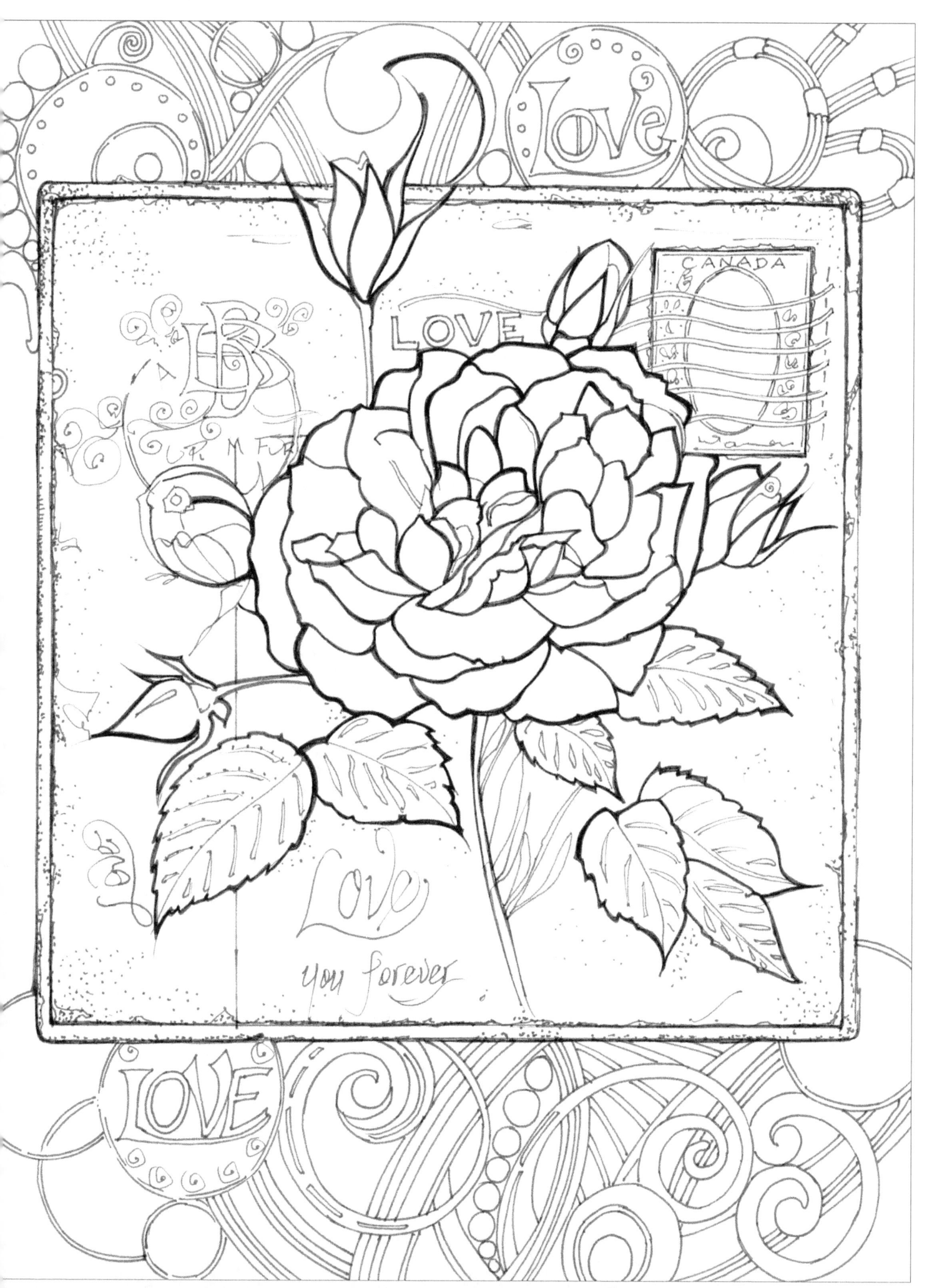

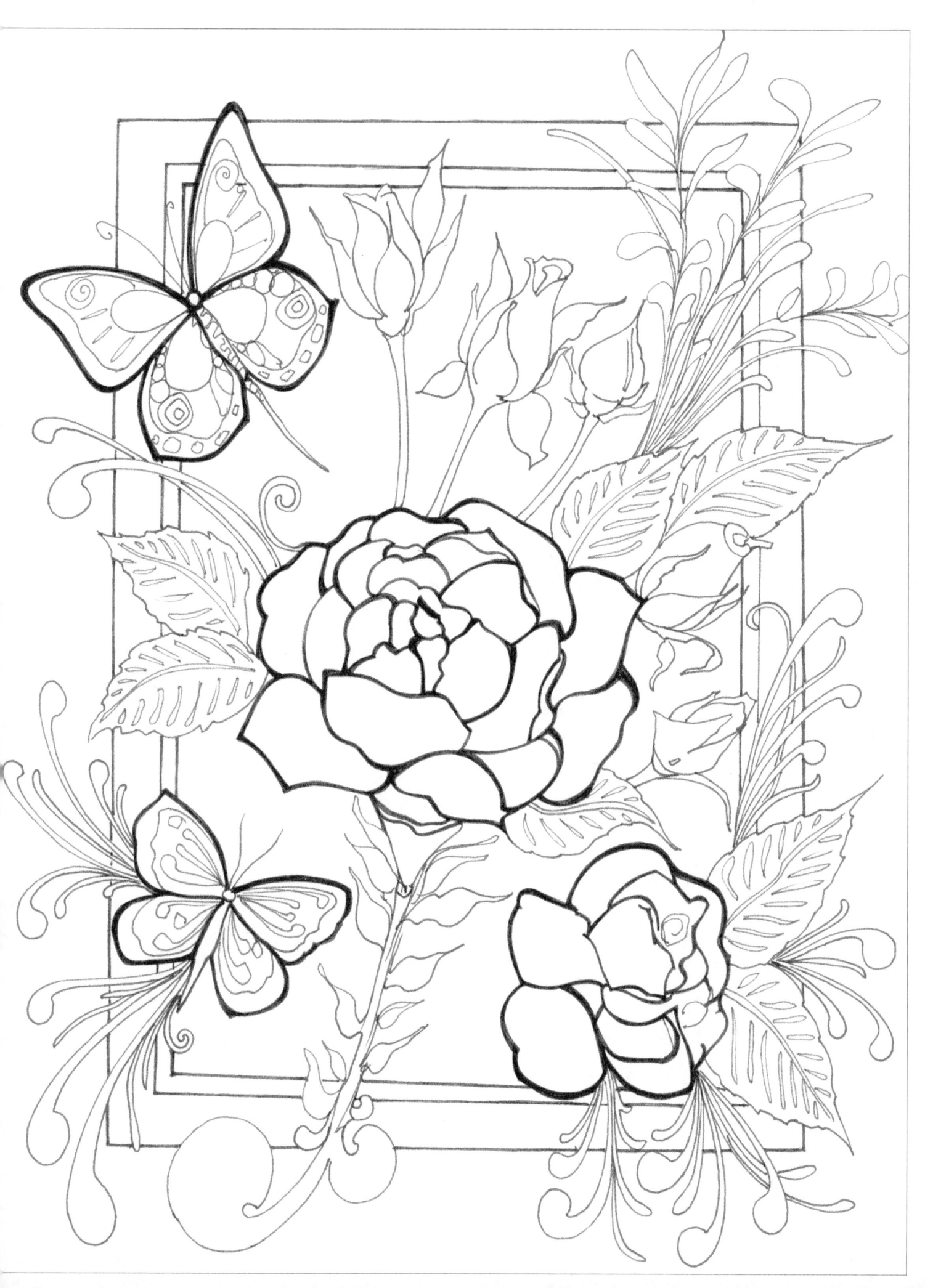

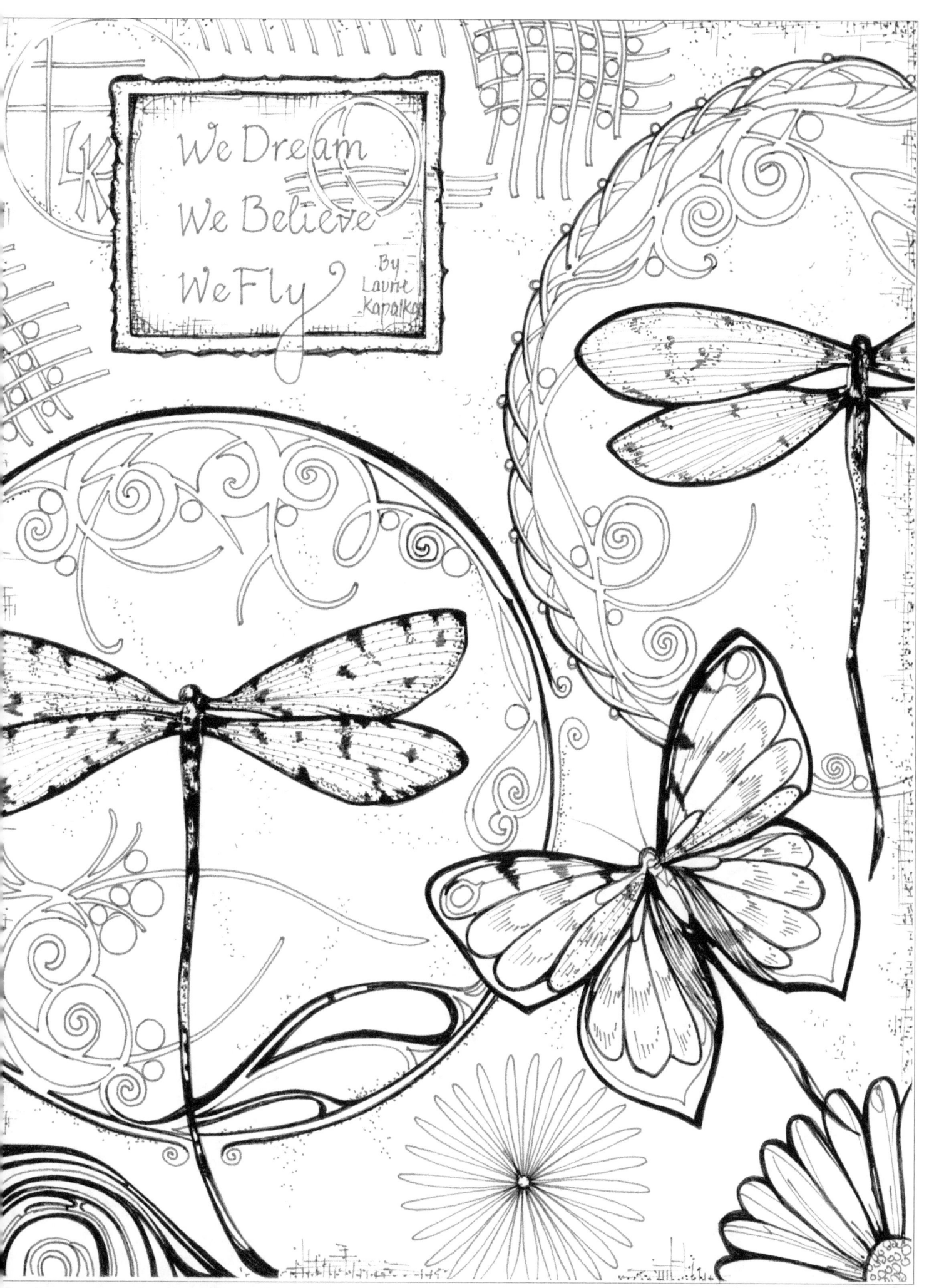

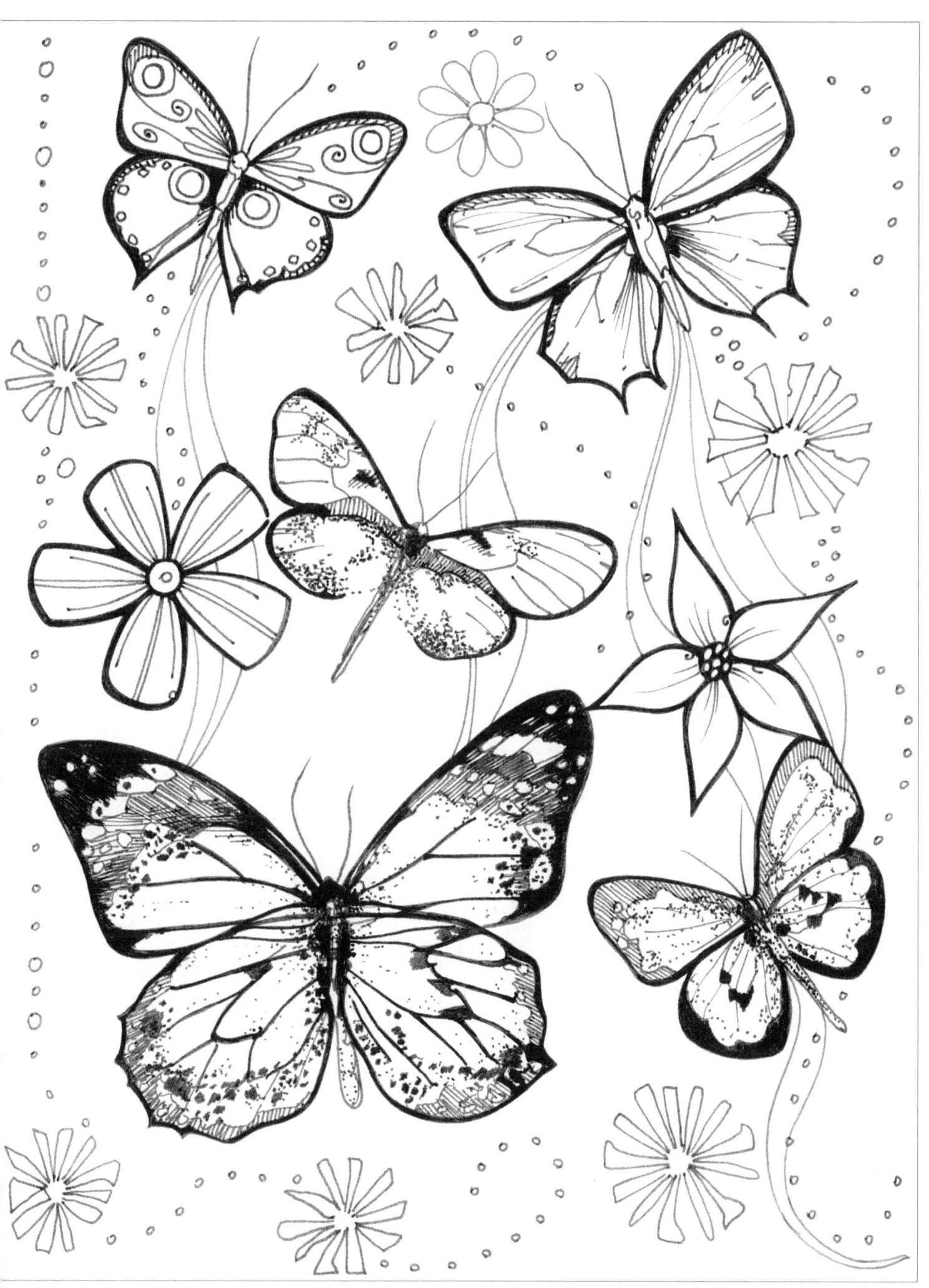

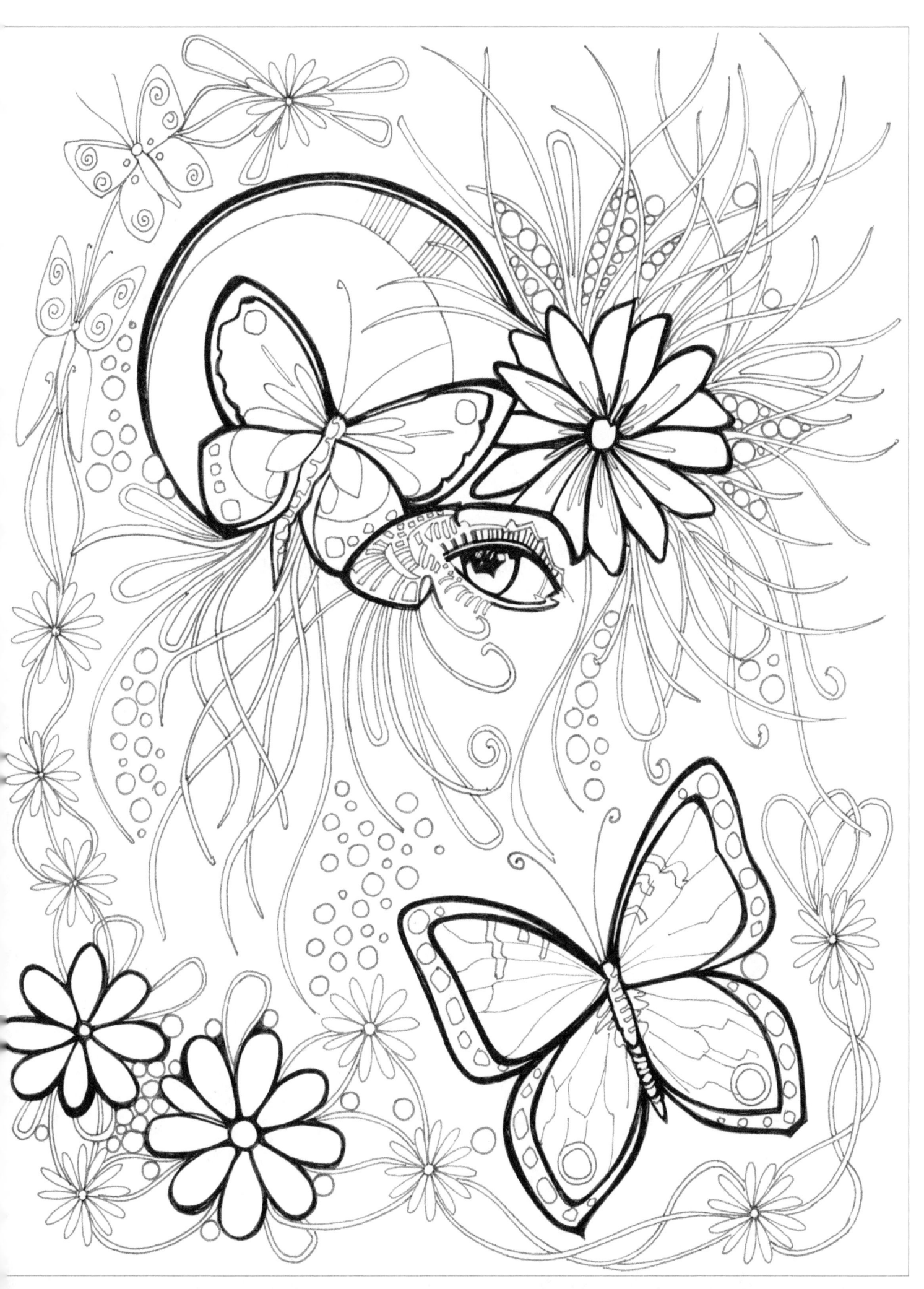

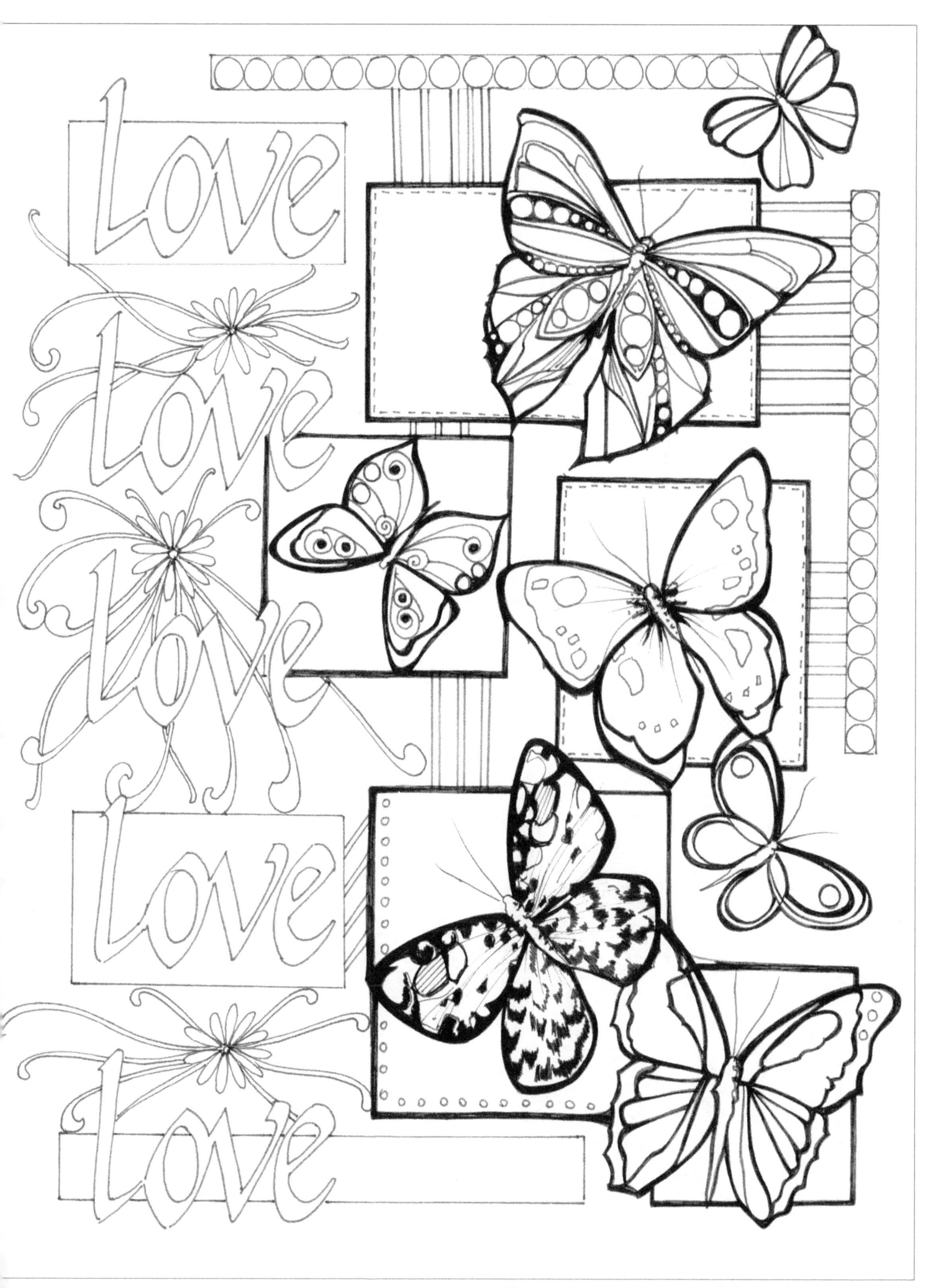

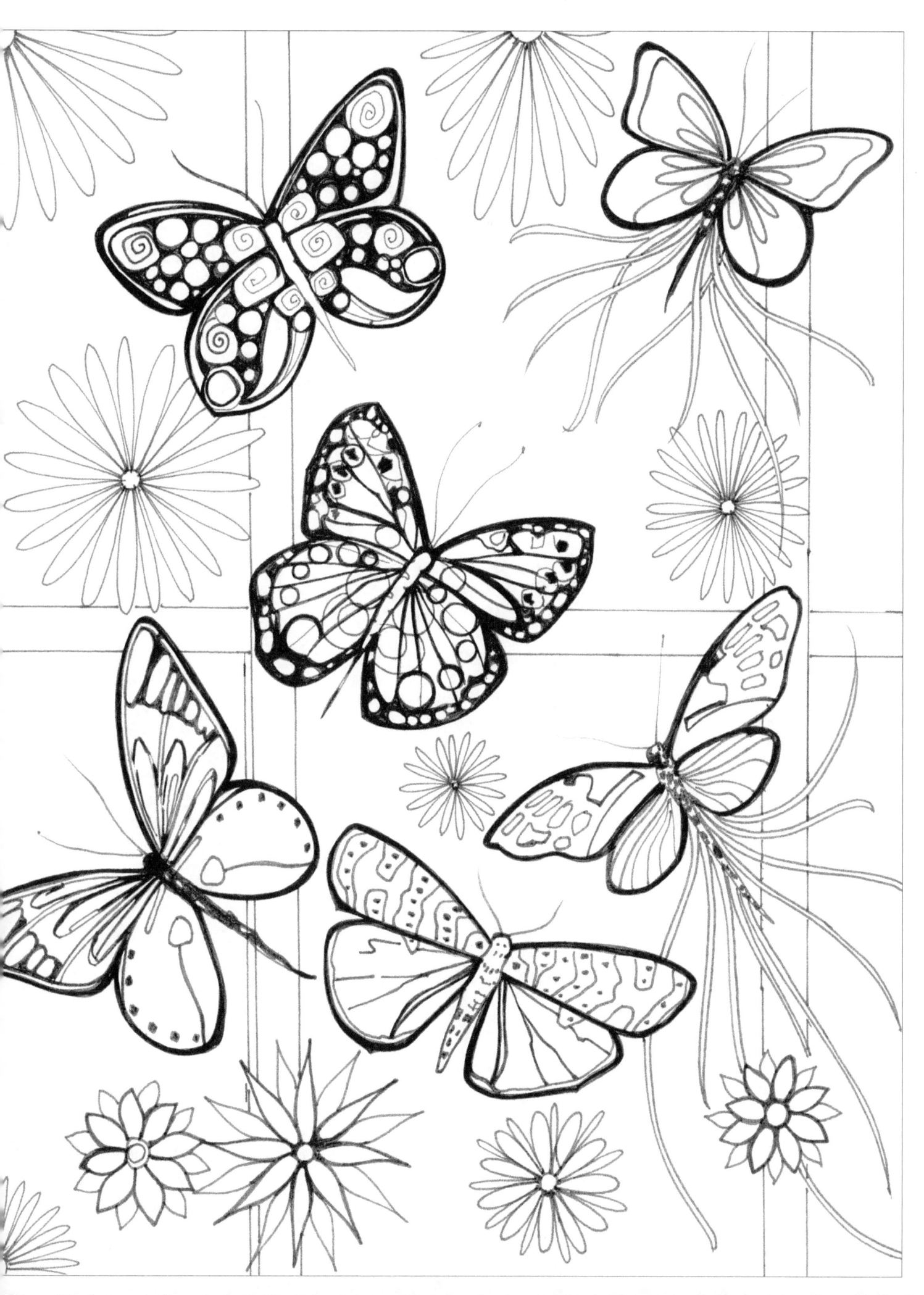

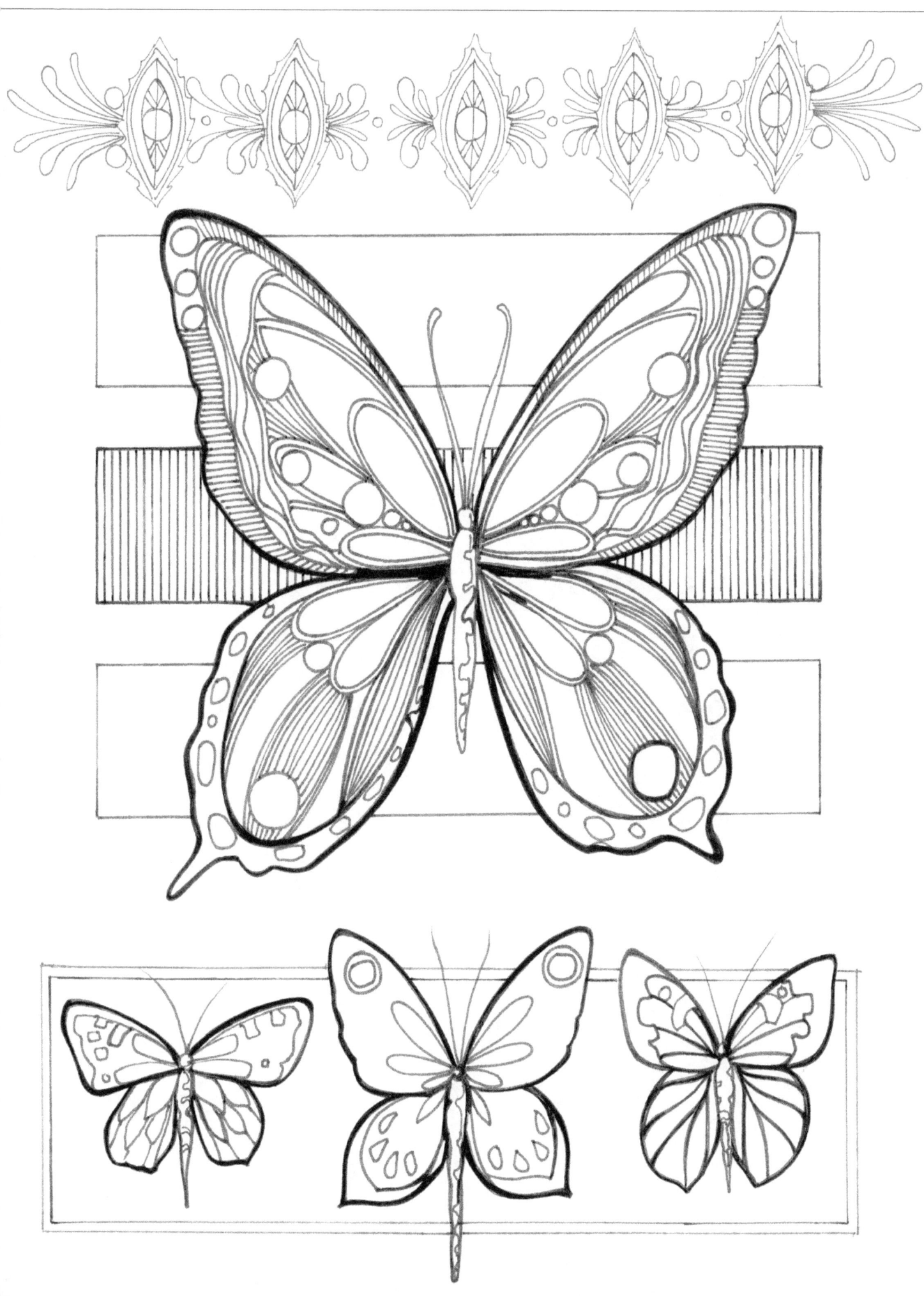

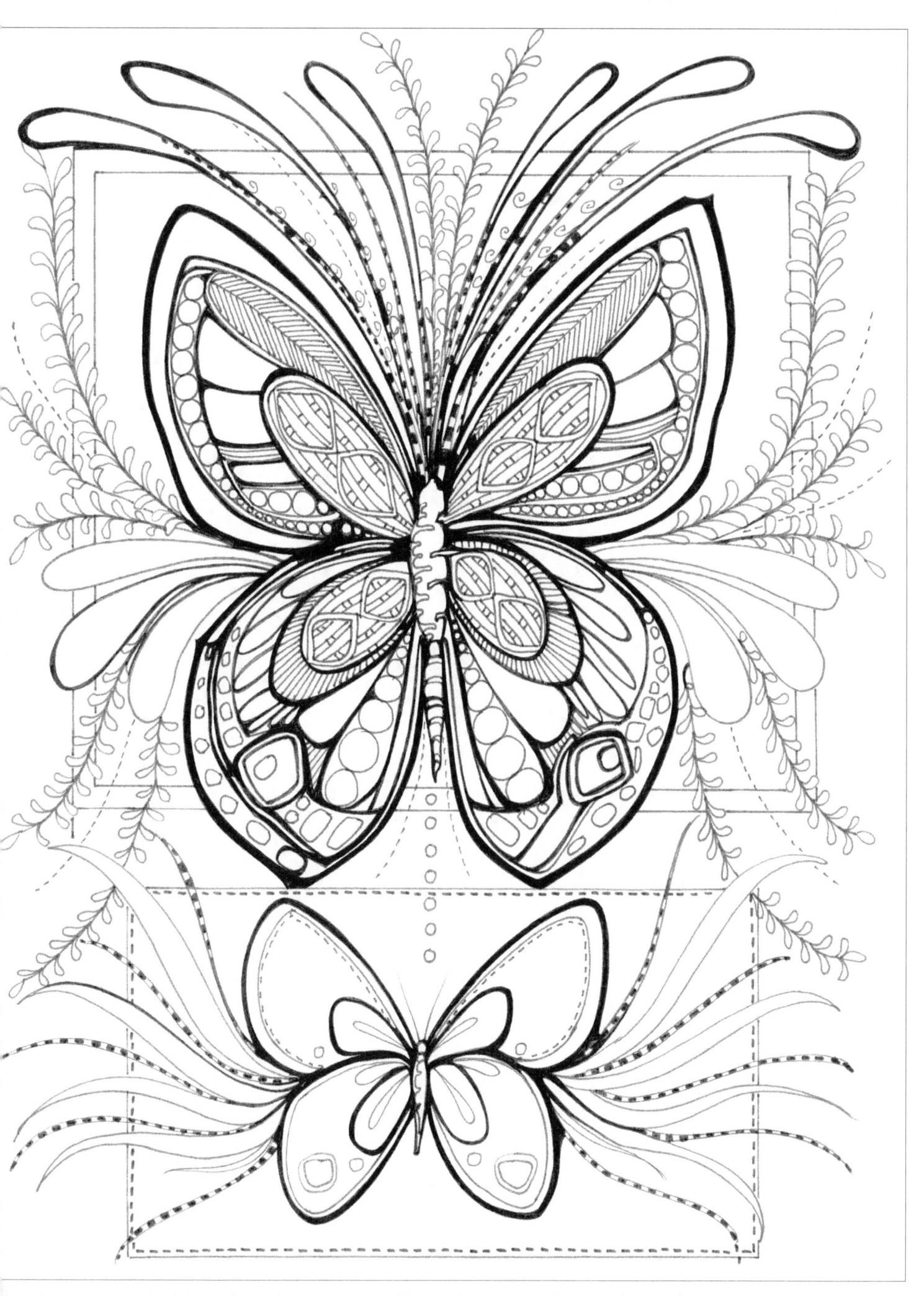

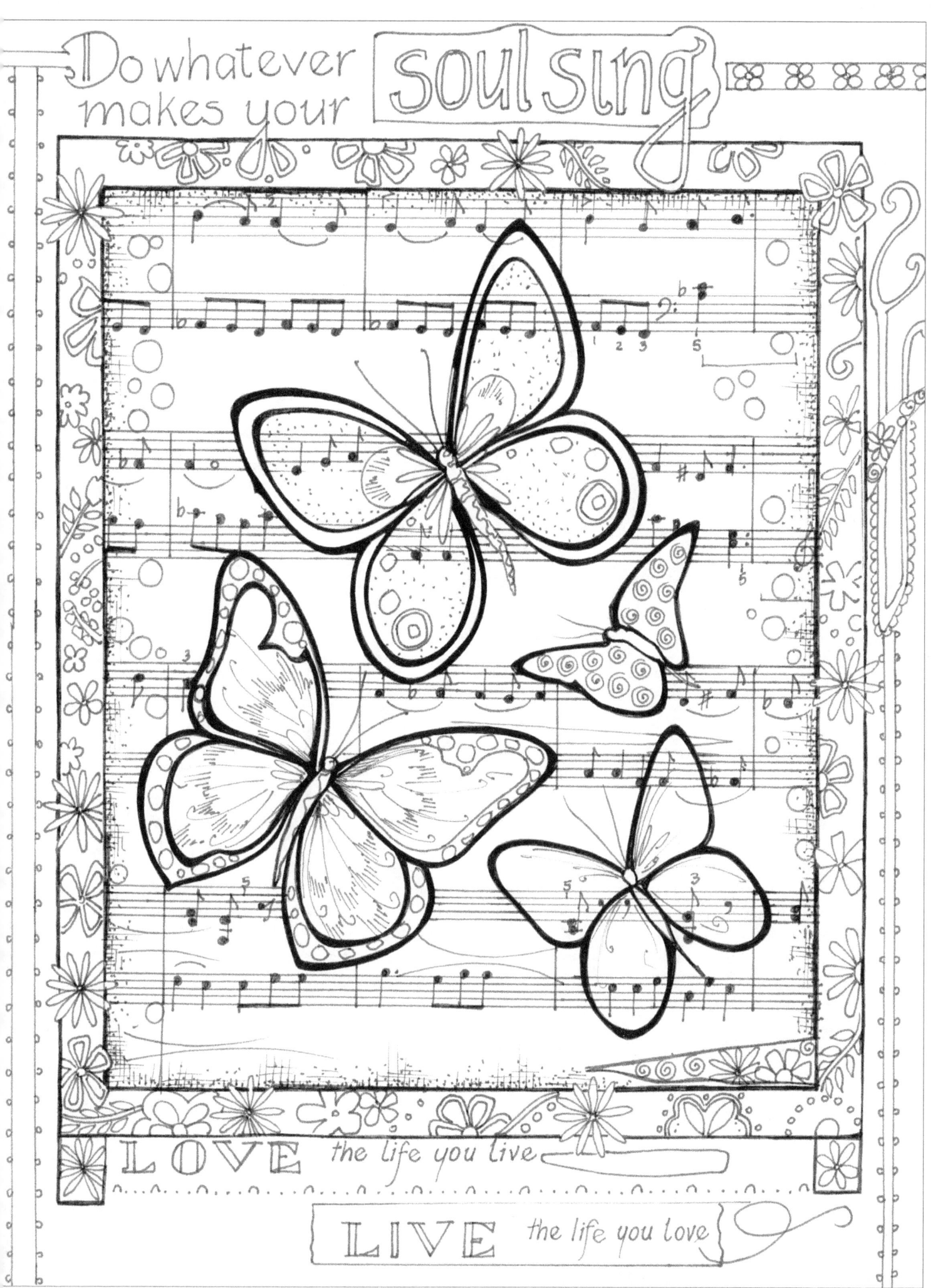

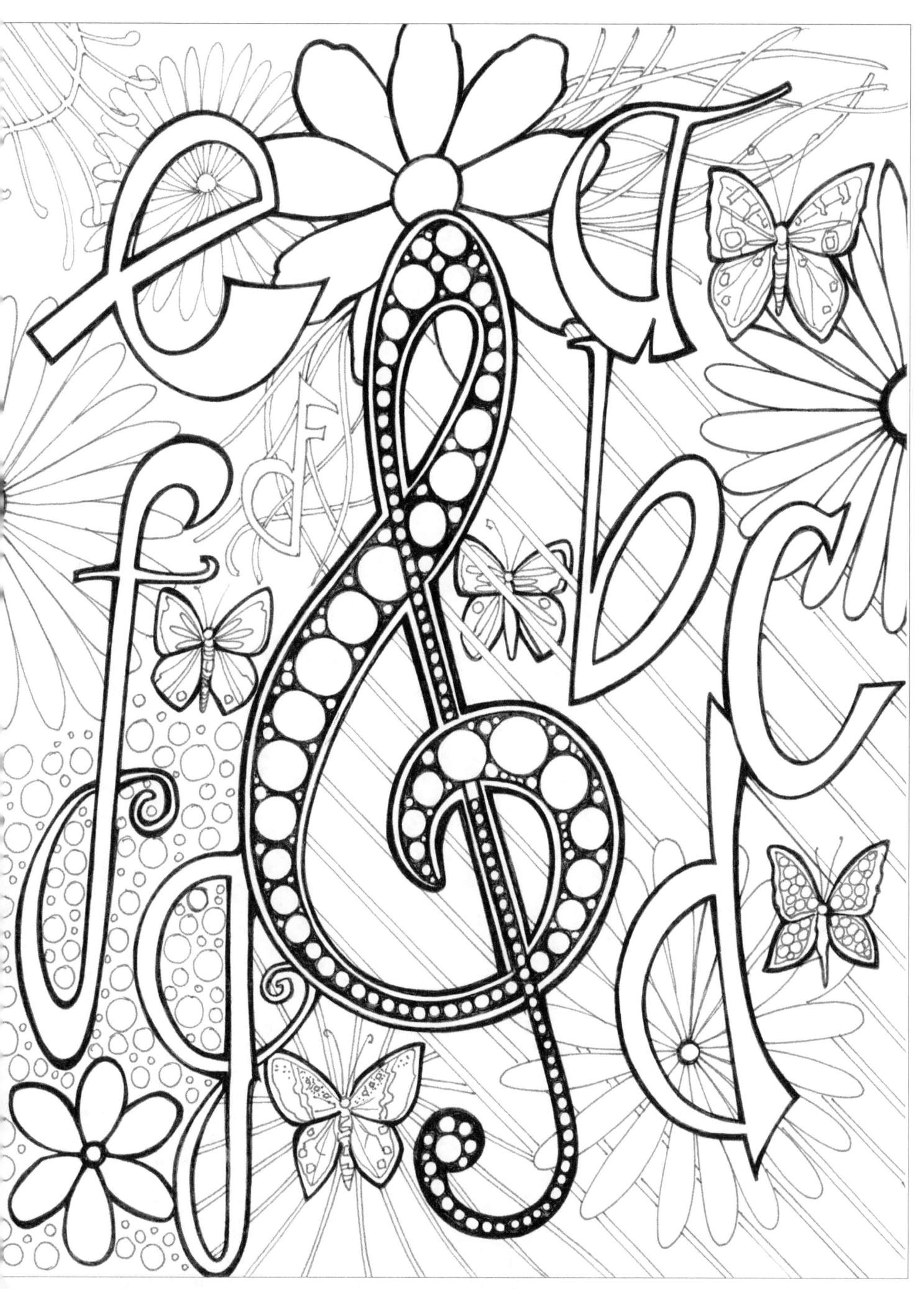

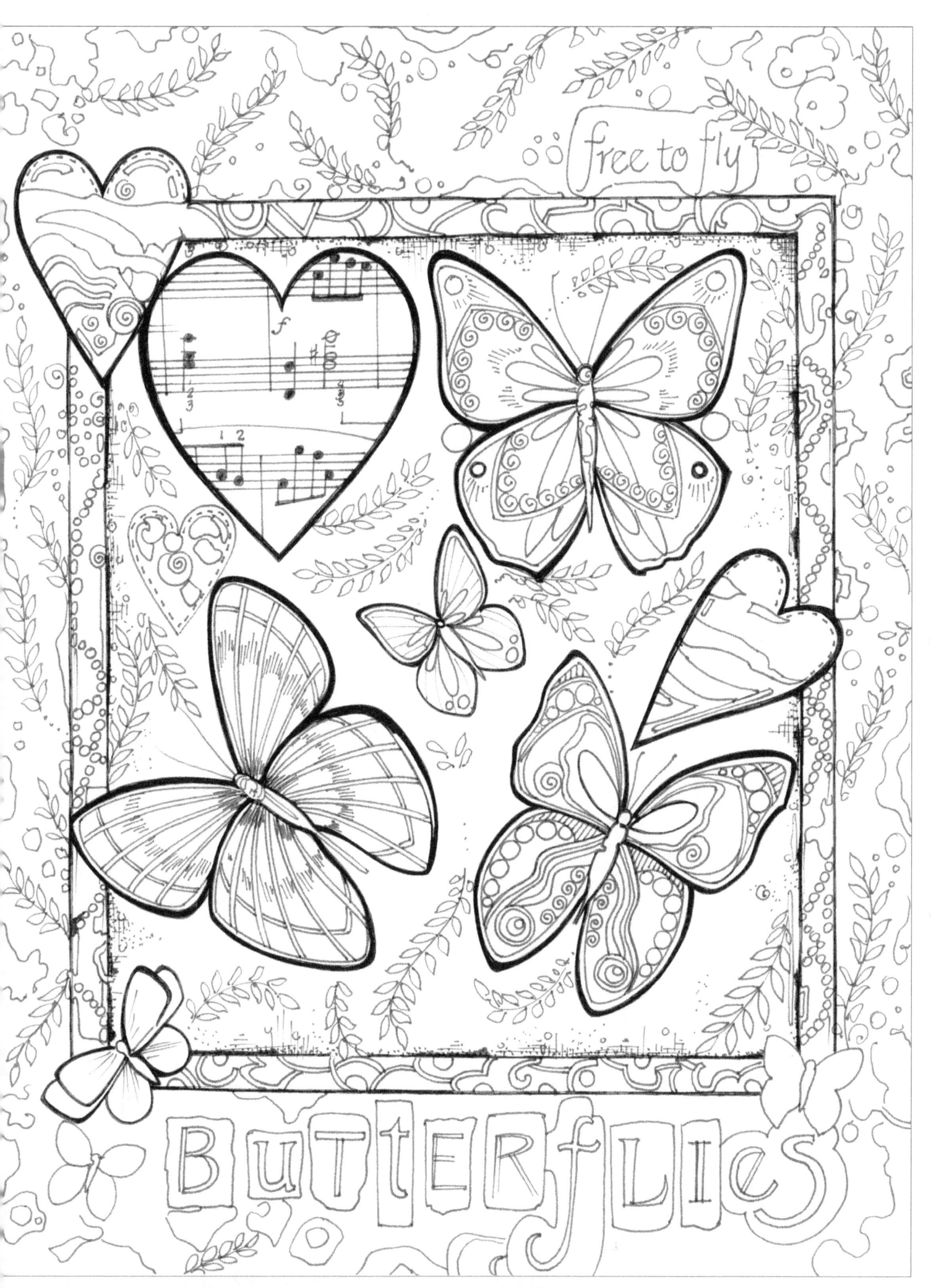

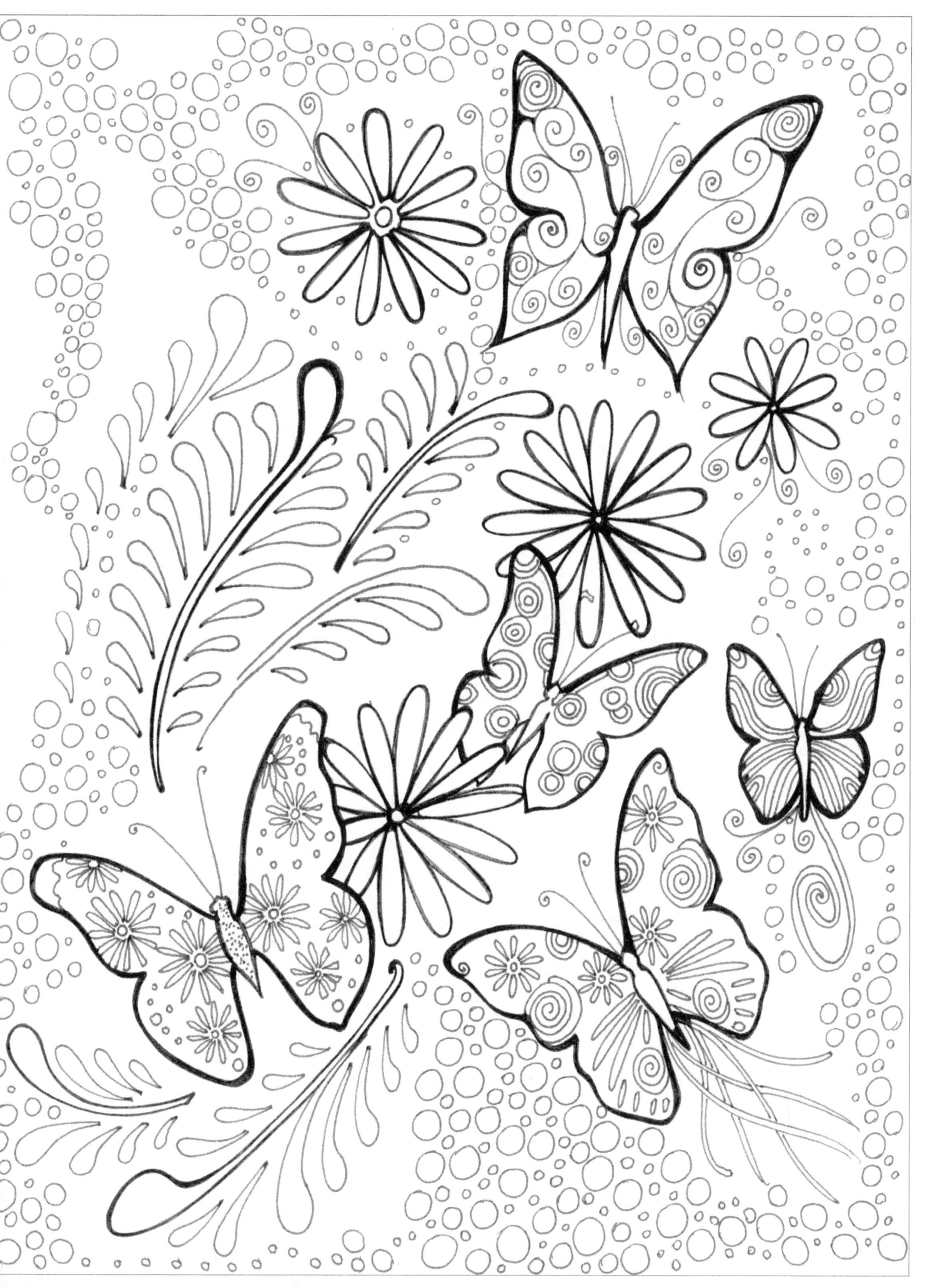

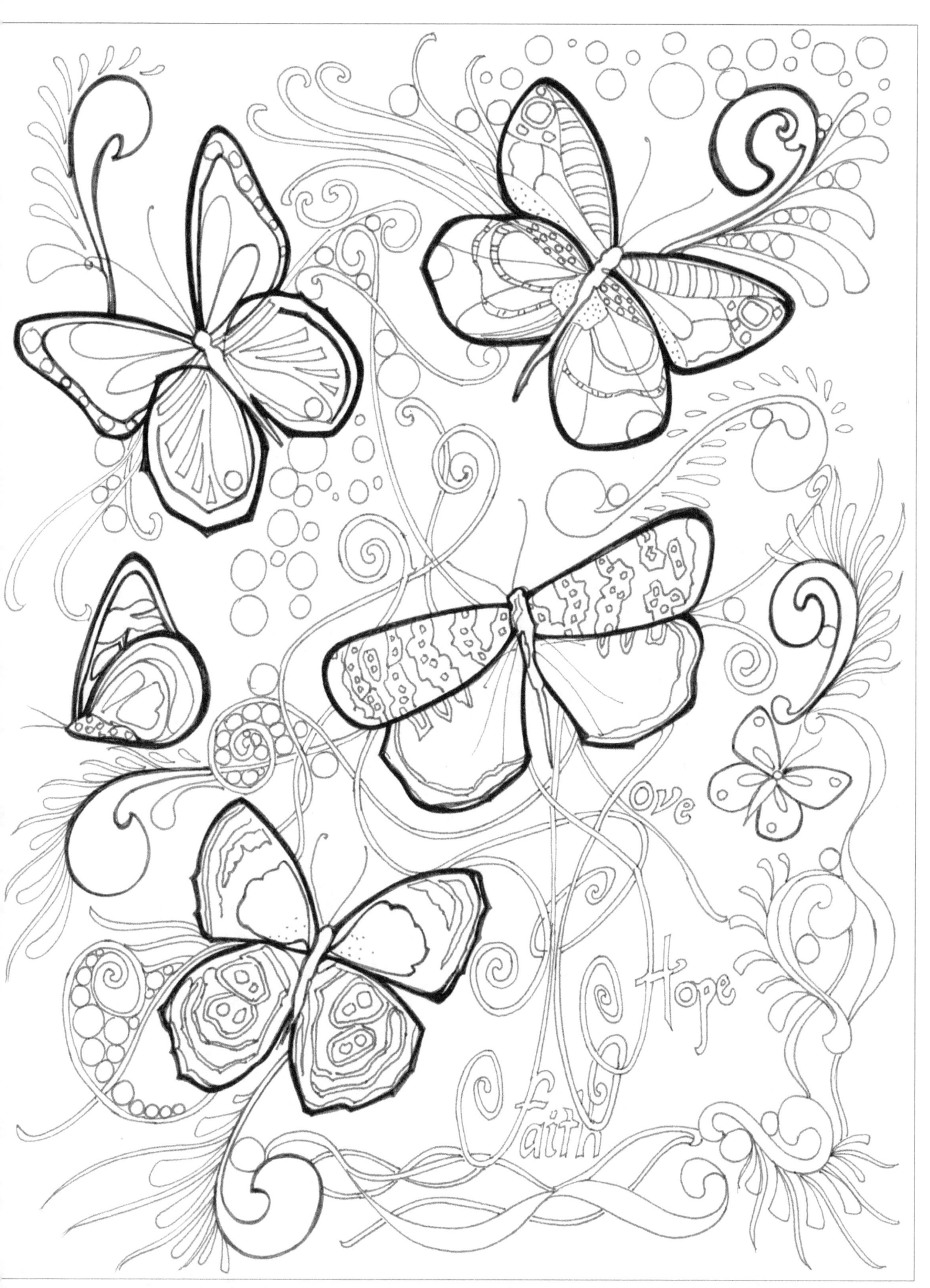

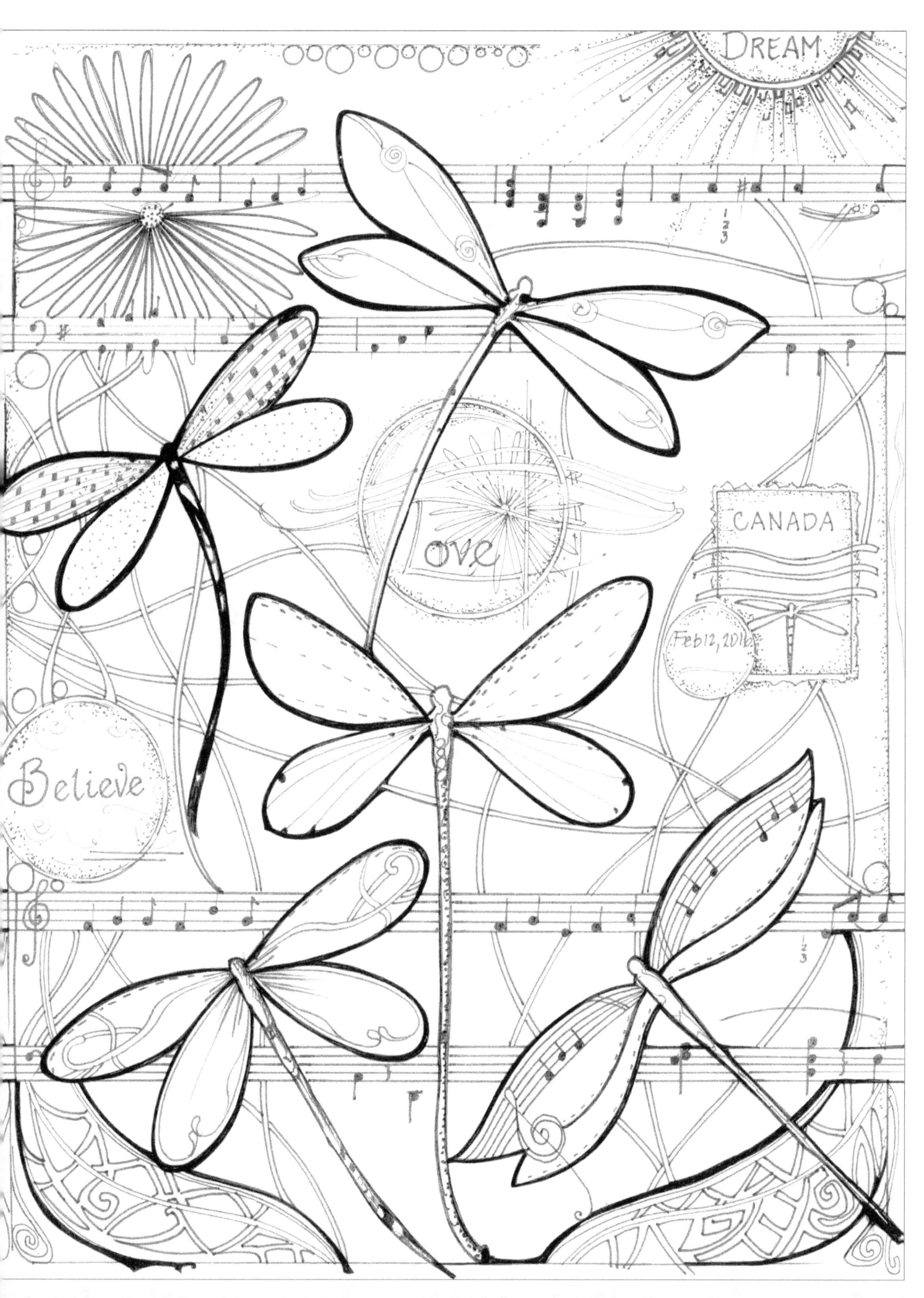

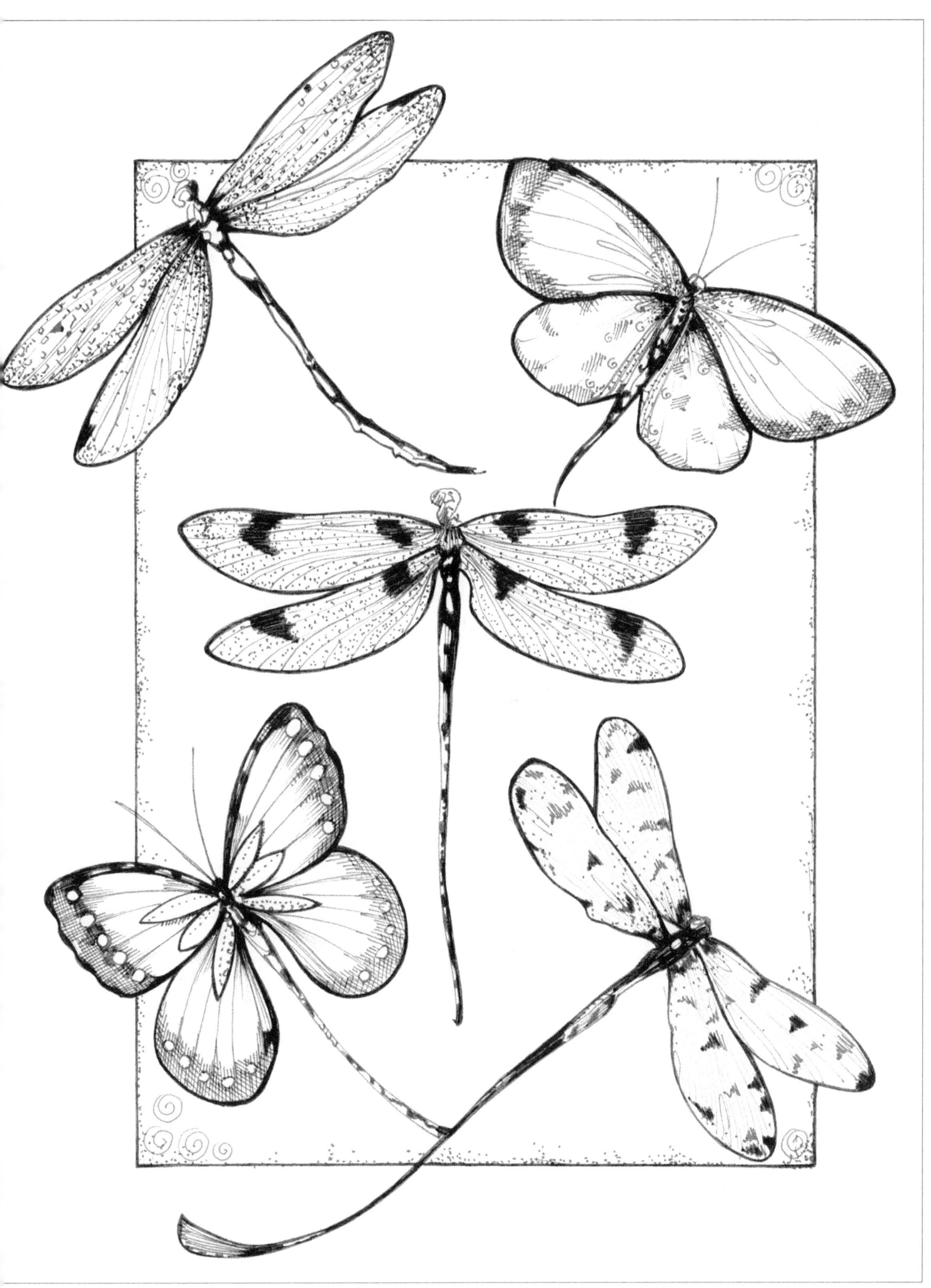

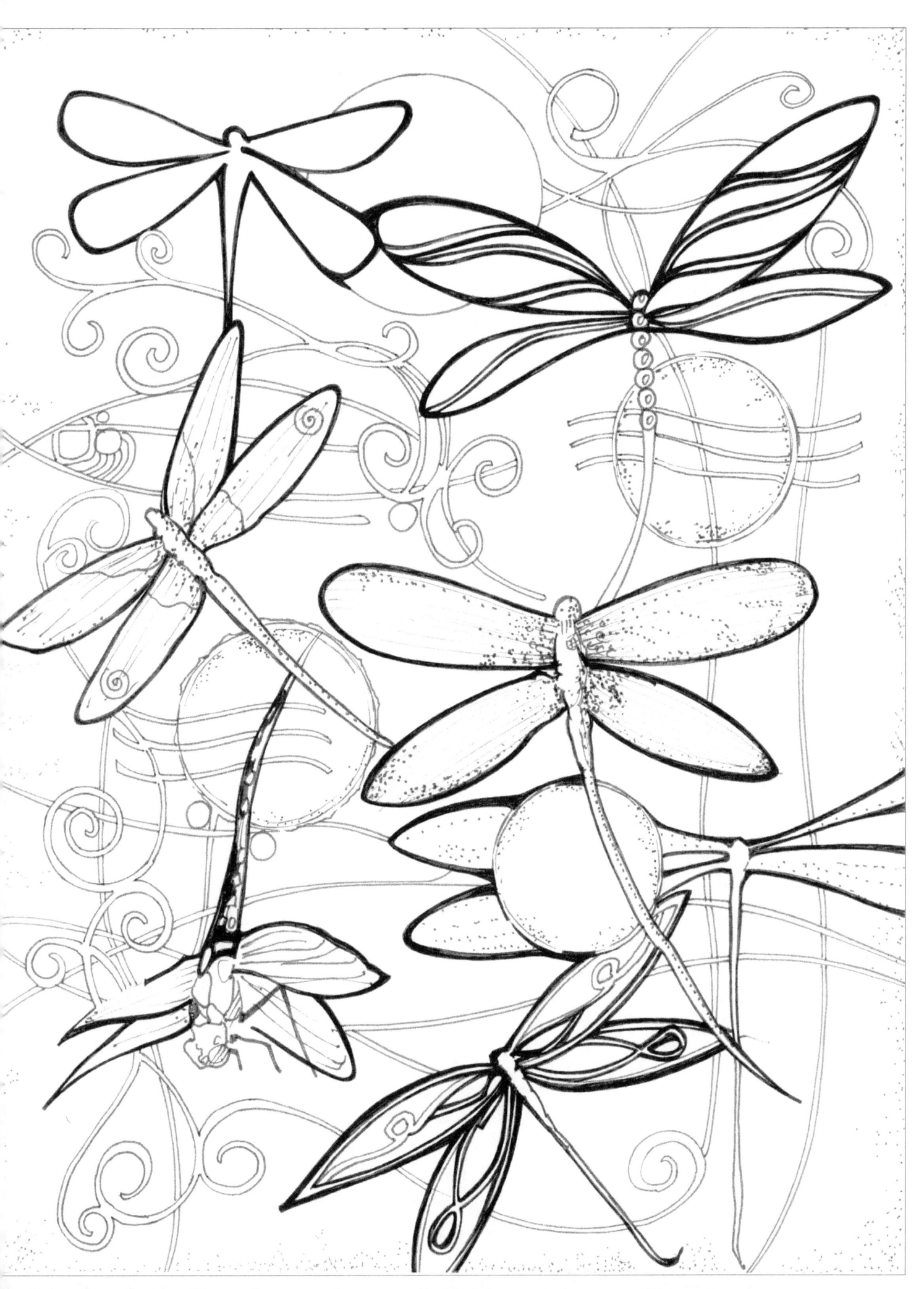

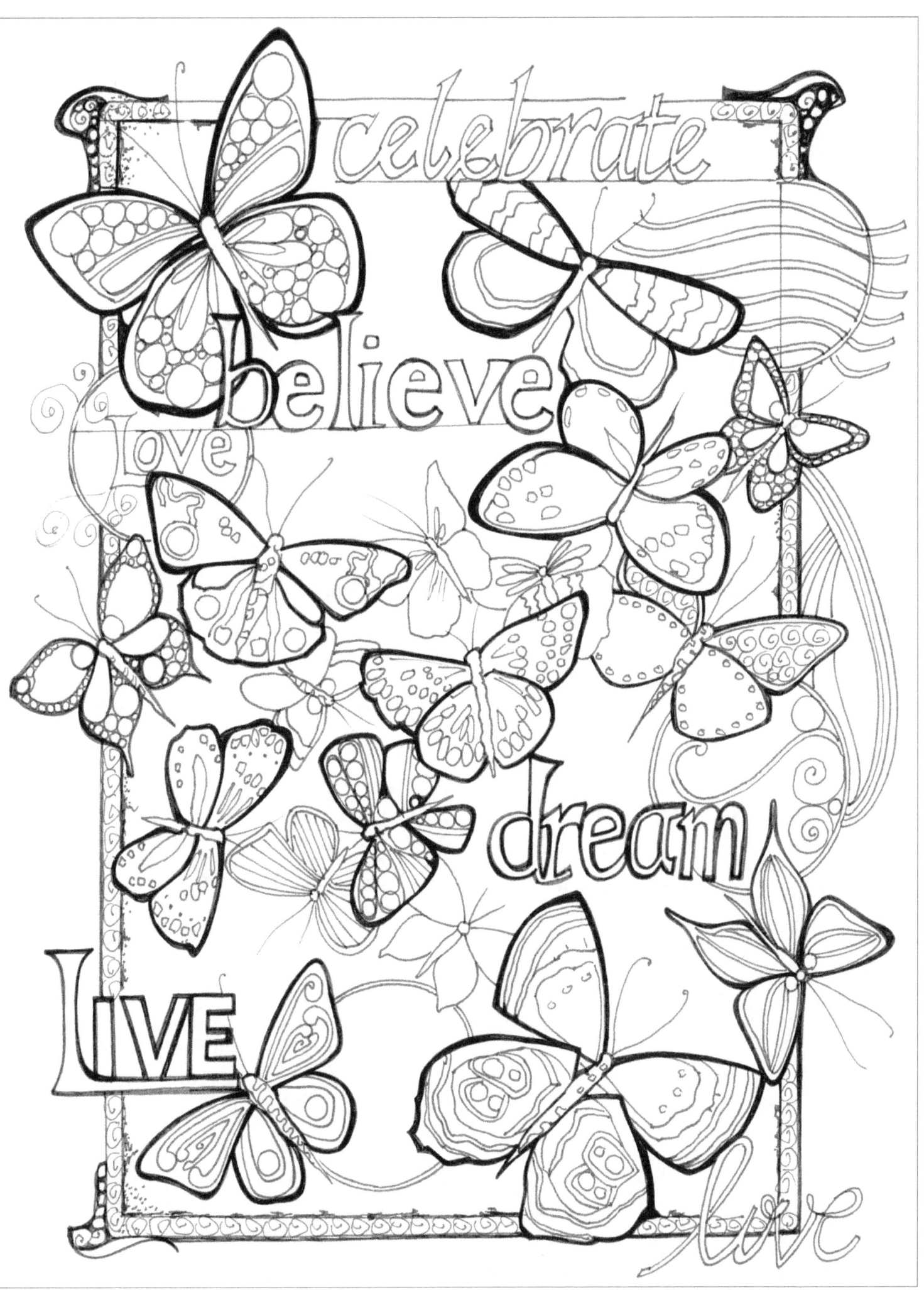

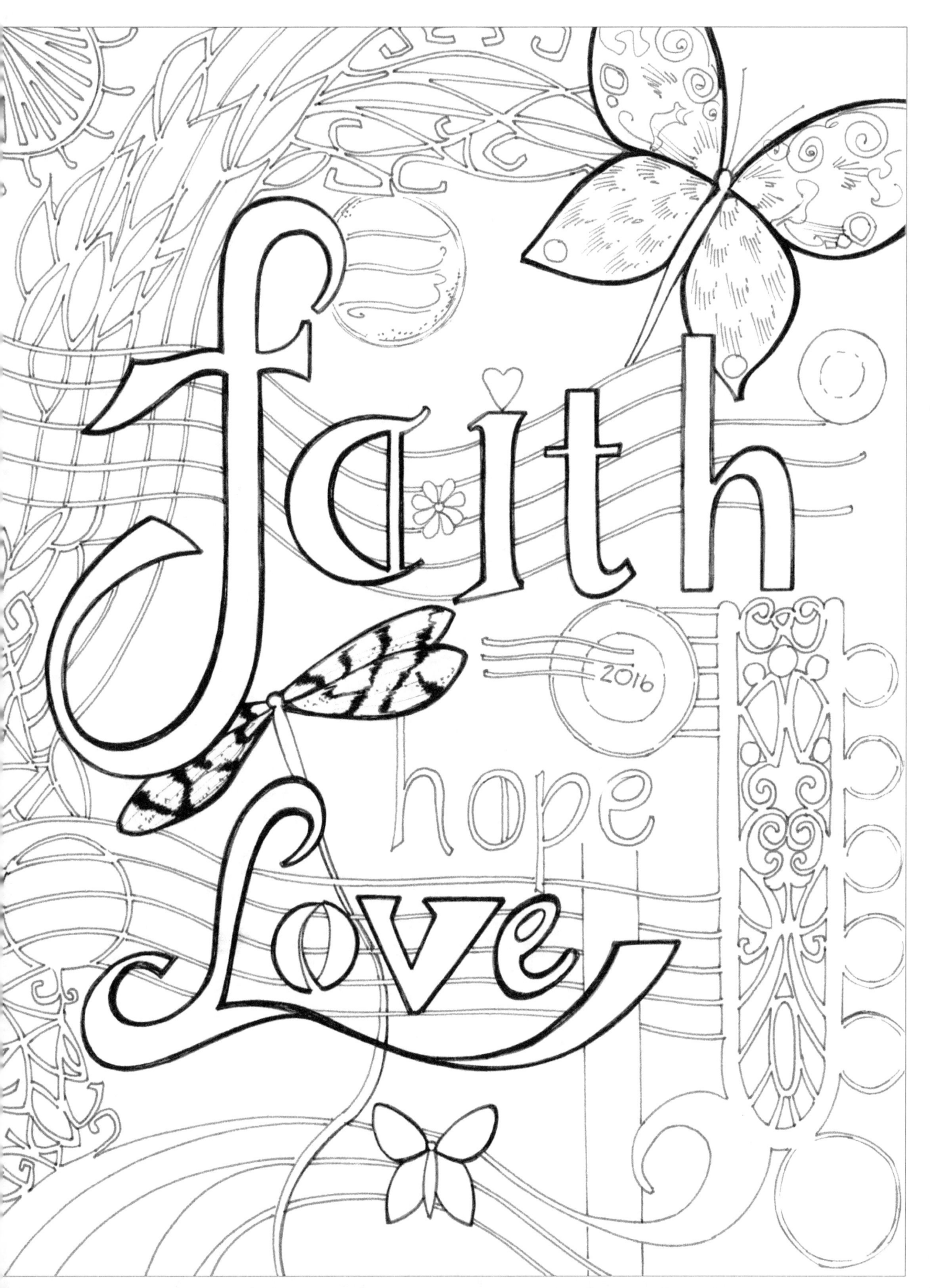

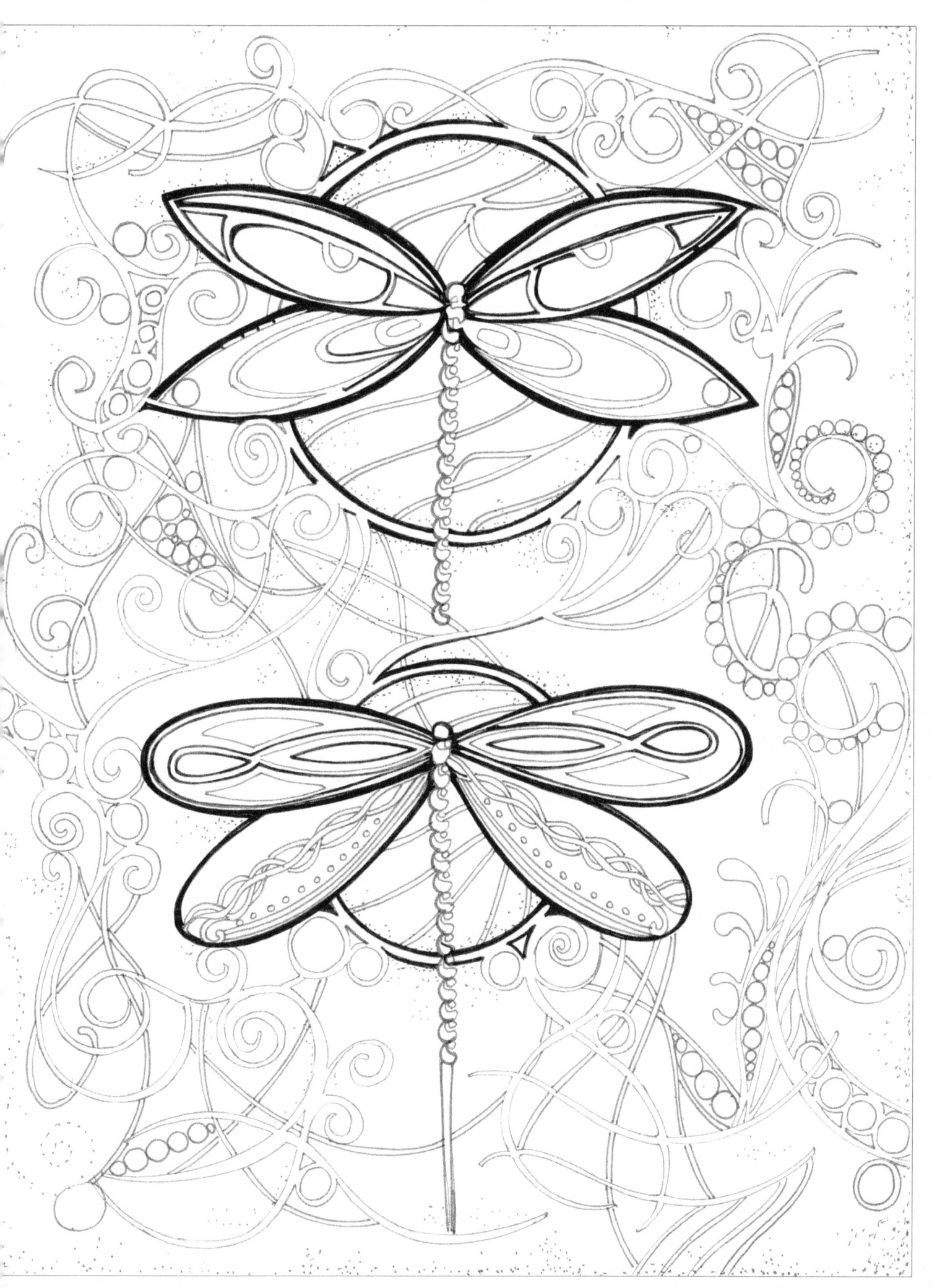

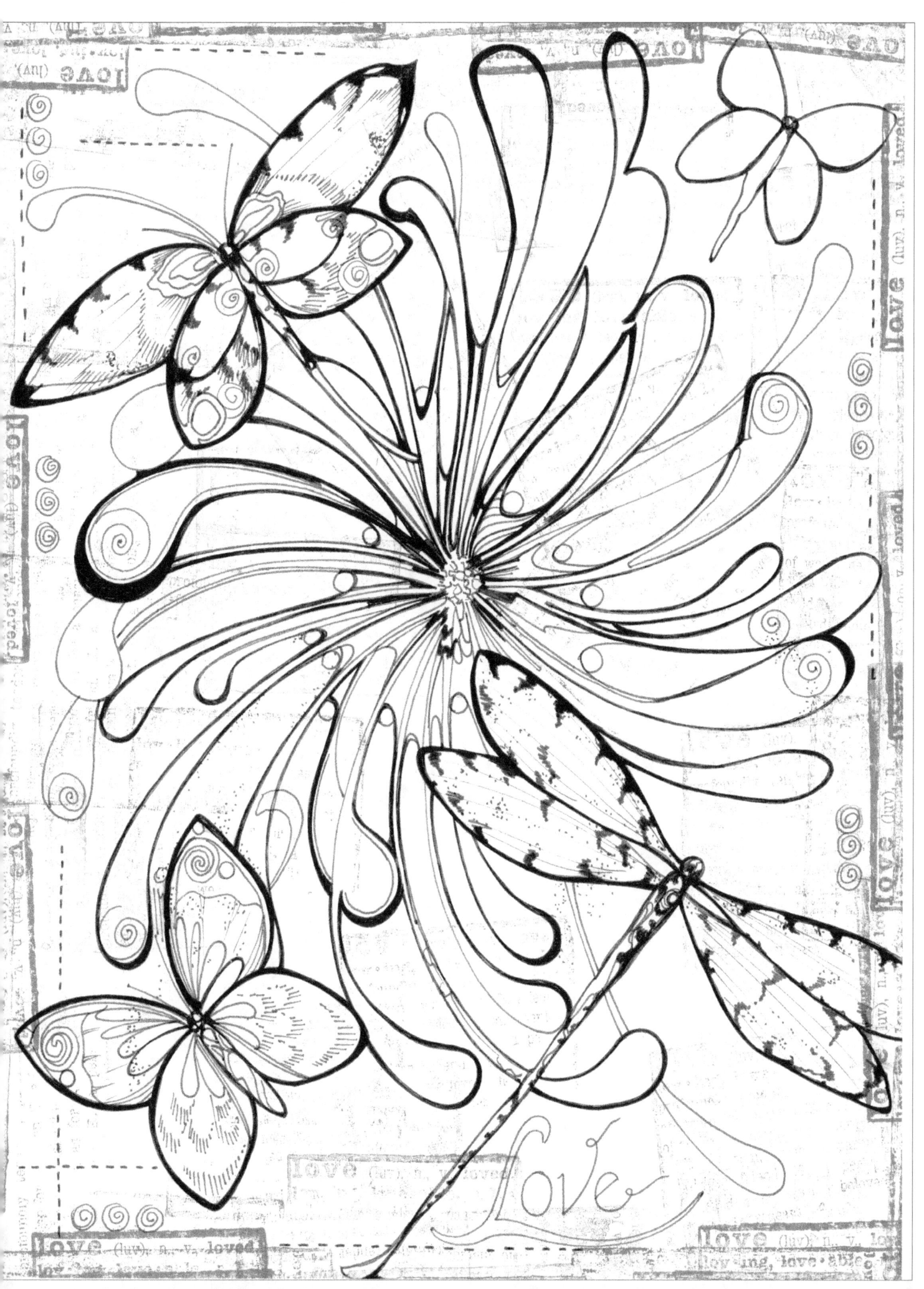

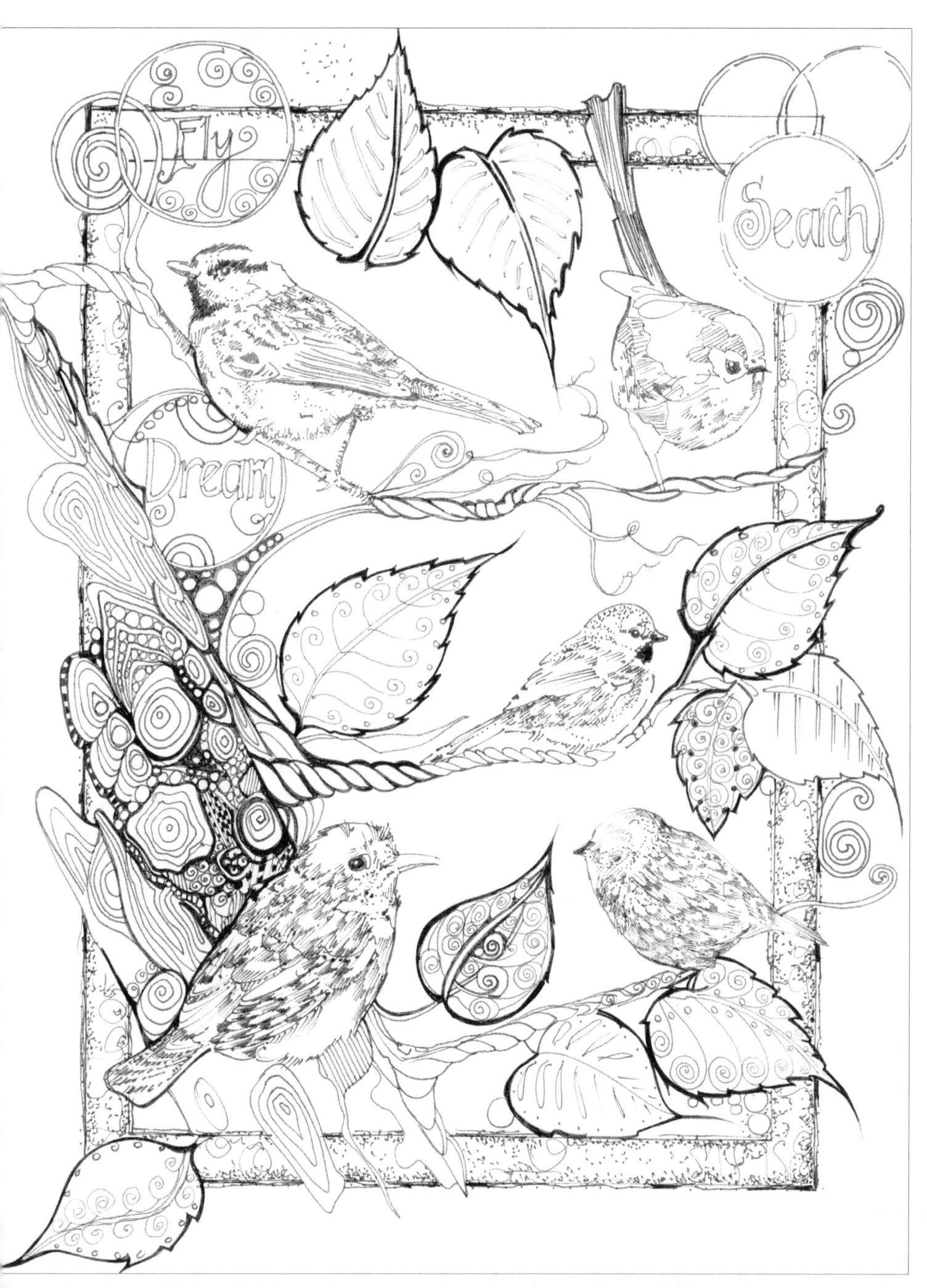

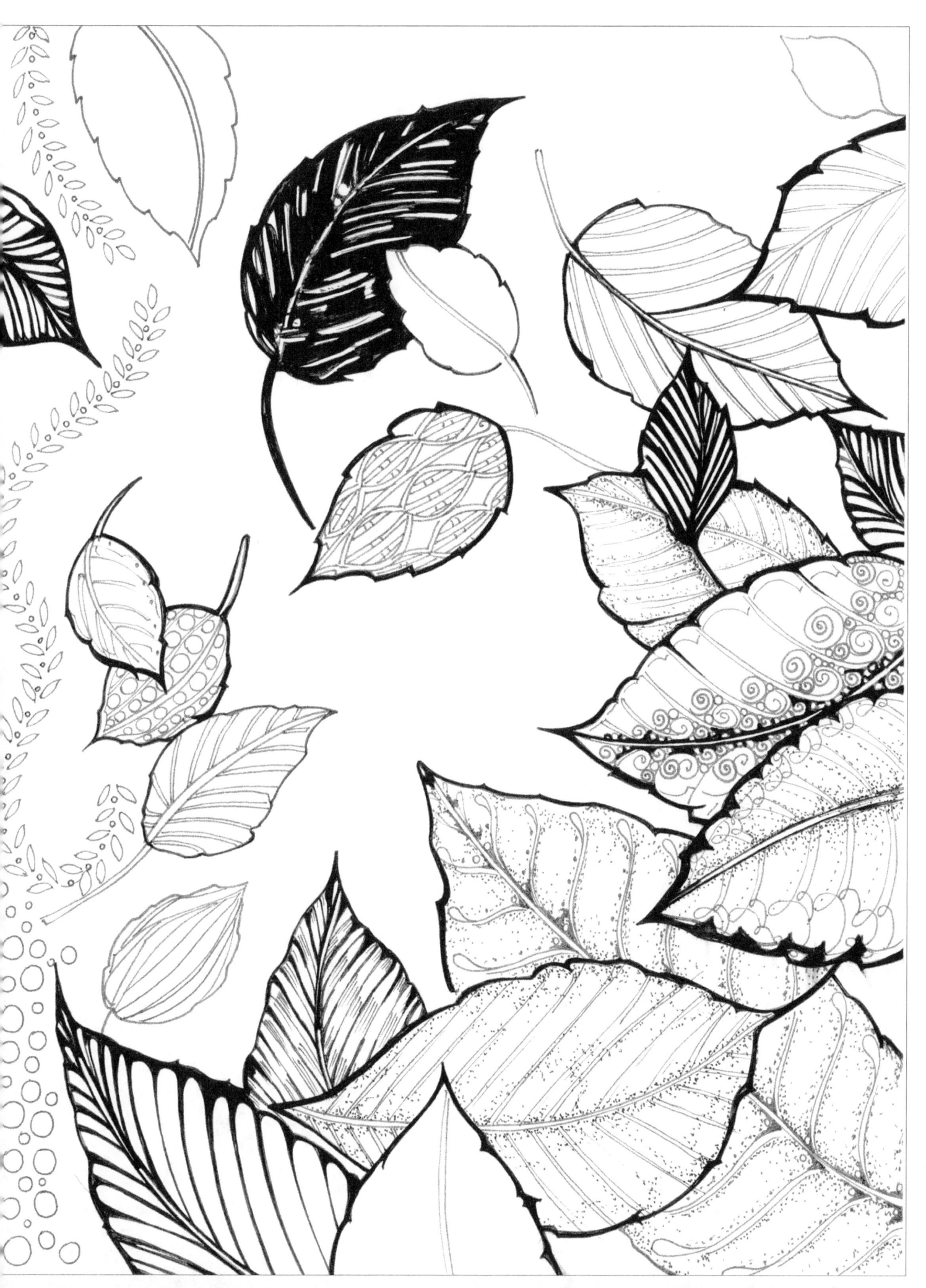

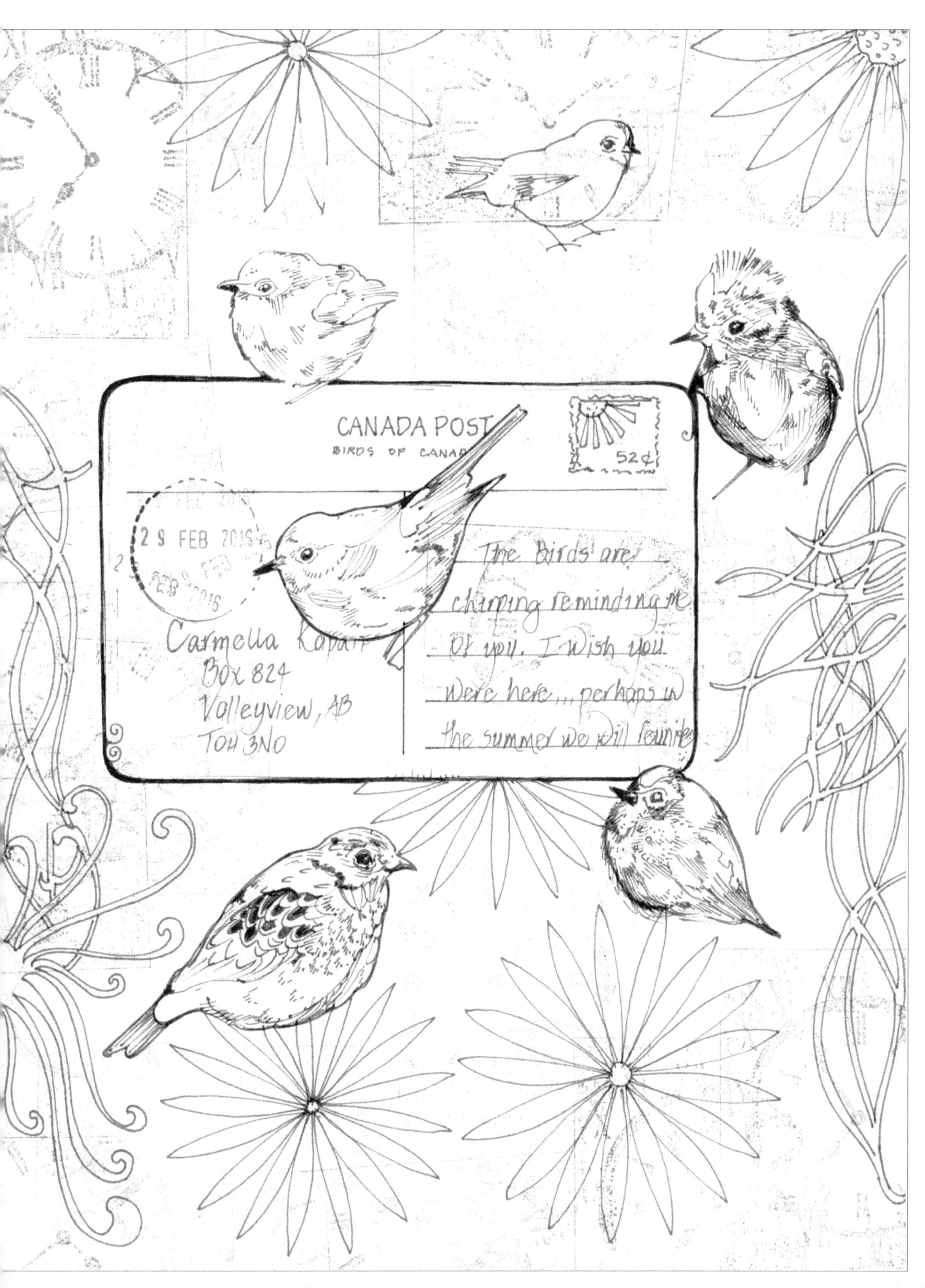

CANADA POST
BIRDS OF CANADA

52¢

29 FEB 2016

Carmella Rabart
Box 824
Valleyview, AB
T0H 3N0

The Birds are
chirping reminding me
of you. I wish you
were here... perhaps in
the summer we will reunite

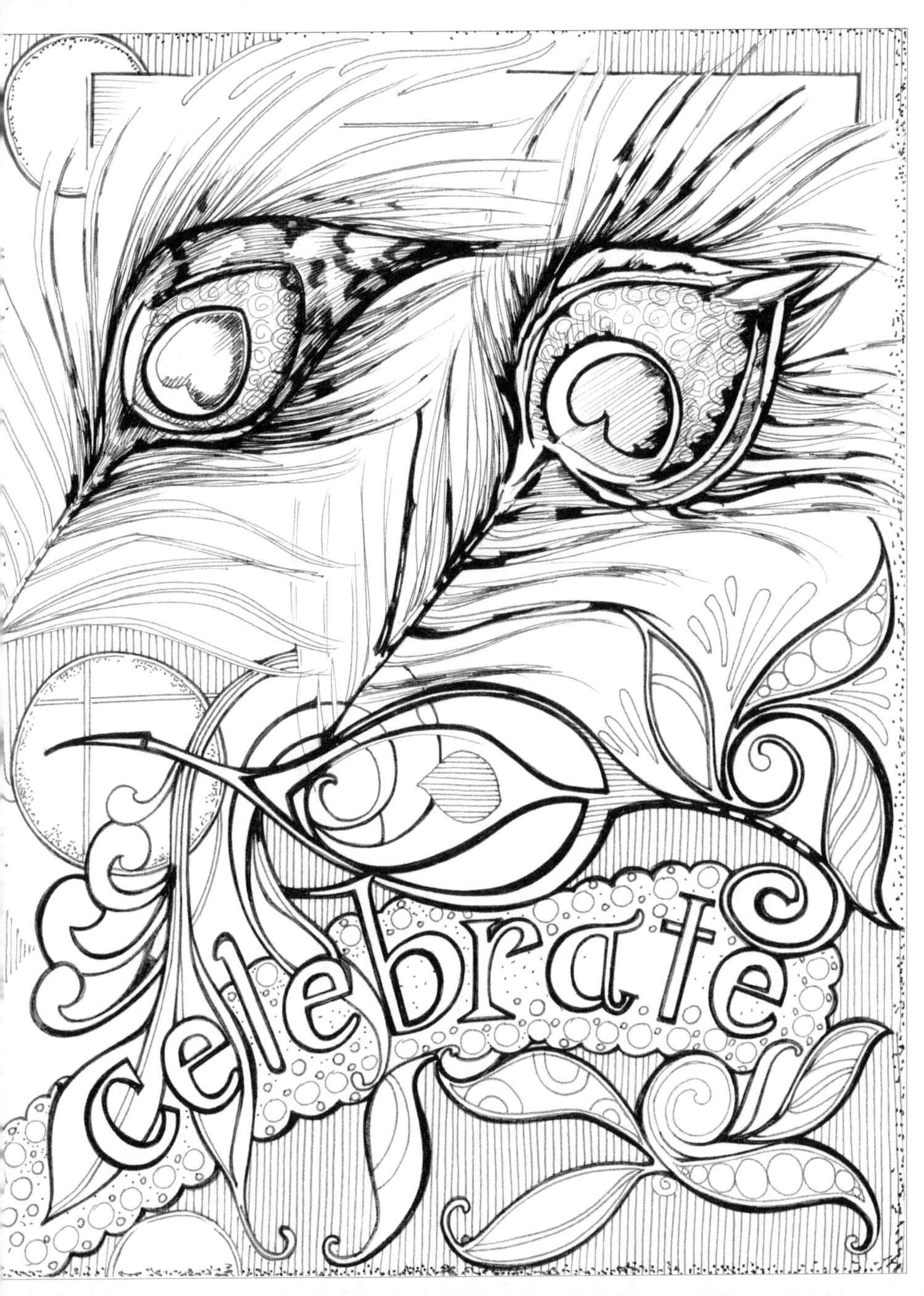

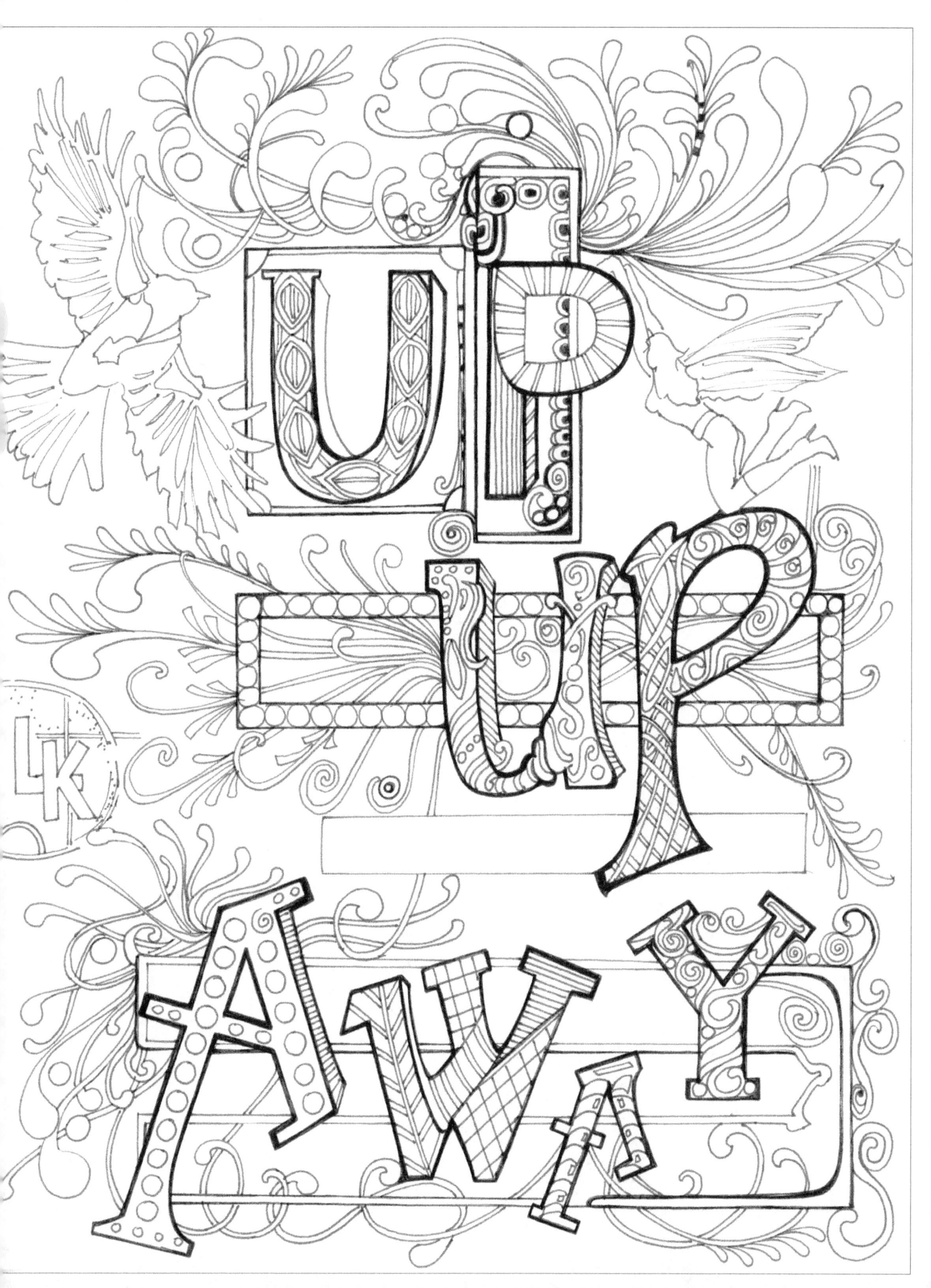

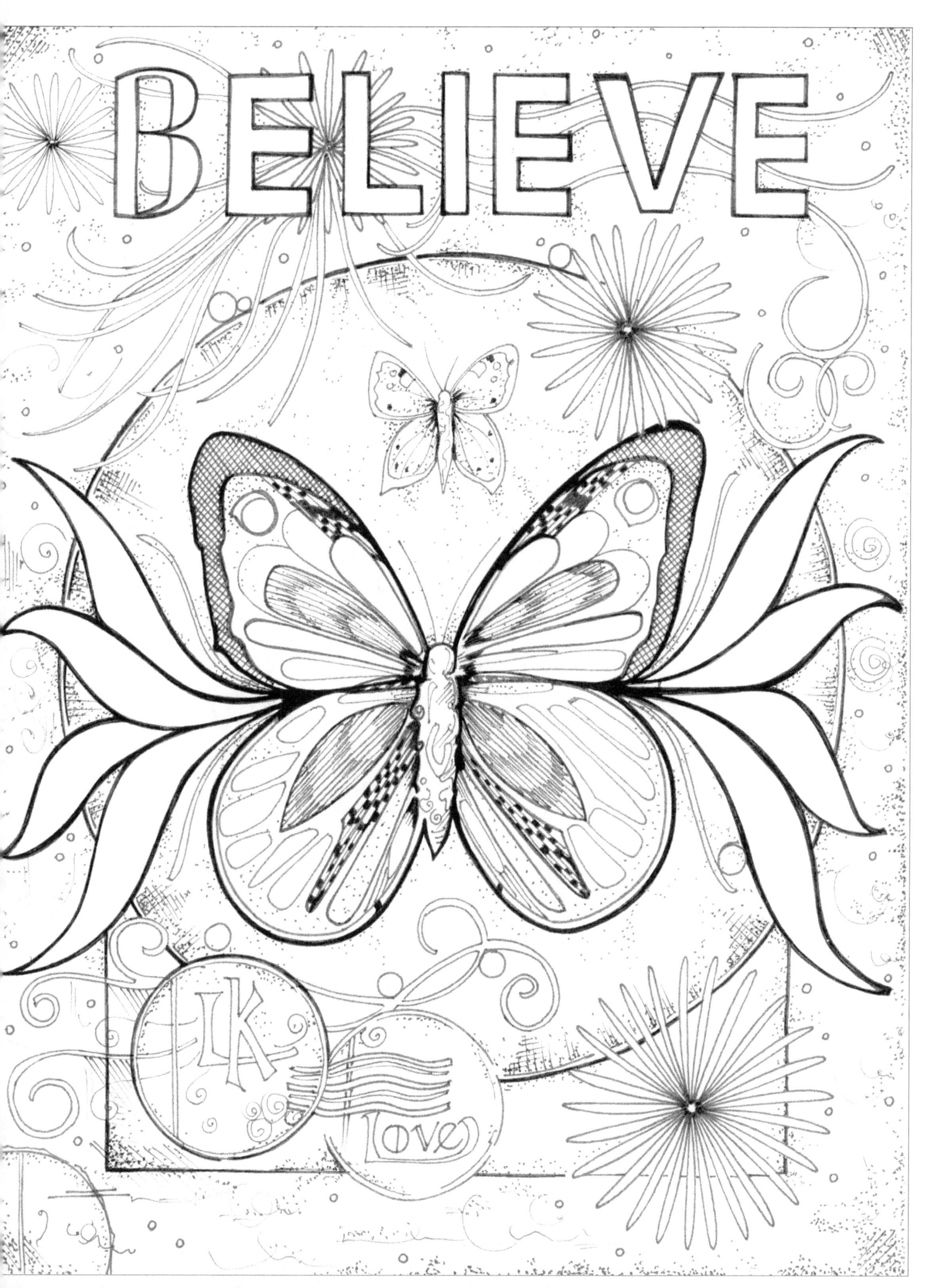